The USS *Flier*

The USS *Flier*

Death and Survival
on a
World War II
Submarine

MICHAEL STURMA

THE UNIVERSITY PRESS OF KENTUCKY

Editorial and Sales Offices: The University Press of Kentucky
663 South Limestone Street, Lexington, Kentucky 40508-4008
www.kentuckypress.com

12 11 10 09 08   5 4 3 2 1

Maps by Dick Gilbreath

Library of Congress Cataloging-in-Publication Data

Sturma, Michael, 1950-
  The USS Flier : death and survival on a World War II submarine / Michael Sturma.
      p. cm.
  Includes bibliographical references and index.
  ISBN 978-0-8131-2481-0 (hbk. : alk. paper)
  1. Flier (Submarine) 2. World War, 1939-1945—Naval operations—Submarine.
  3. World War, 1939-1945—Naval operations, American. 4. World War, 1939-
  1945—Campaigns—Pacific Ocean. 5. Survival after airplane accidents,
  shipwrecks, etc.—Philippines—Palawan. I. Title.
  D783.5.F56S88 2008
  940.54'510973—dc22   2007046559

This book is printed on acid-free recycled paper meeting the requirements of the American National Standard for Permanence in Paper for Printed Library Materials.

Manufactured in the United States of America.

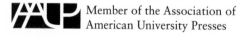 Member of the Association of
American University Presses

To Joan Roberts

Contents

Acknowledgments

Numerous people assisted in the research for this study. Charles Hinman and Nancy Richards extended the aloha spirit at the USS *Bowfin* Submarine Museum at Pearl Harbor. My special thanks to Charles for his lunchtime conversations and his Web site On Eternal Patrol. I am grateful to Steve Finnigan and Wendy Gulley for their assistance at the Submarine Force Museum at Groton, Connecticut. Carol Bowers and John Waggener of the American Heritage Center at Laramie provided invaluable help both at a distance and on the spot. Kathleen Lloyd of the Naval Historical Center, P. A. Leonard from the Office of the Judge Advocate General, and Patrick Kerwin from the Library of Congress made important contributions in piecing together the USS *Flier*'s history.

I was fortunate to have the logistical help of Susan Witt, Wes Witt, and Barbara Eblen during my research in the United States. Closer to home, my friend and colleague Mike Durey provided a fount of naval knowledge. Peter Marks generously guided me through the Weld Club in Western Australia. Like much of my writing, this project benefited from the support of my wife, Ying.

I owe special thanks to Alvin E. Jacobson for sharing his memoirs and memories. I hope this book will serve as a tribute to the remarkable men of the *Flier*.

Prologue

The thirteenth proved unlucky for the USS *Flier*. On Sunday night, 13 August 1944, the submarine was speeding on the surface through the treacherous waters of Balabac Strait between Borneo and the Philippine island of Palawan. At 10:00 P.M. an explosion came without warning. In less than sixty seconds the submarine was plummeting toward the bottom of the ocean, leaving only fourteen of the crew struggling on the surface. After nearly eighteen hours in the water, eight men made it to land in enemy territory.

The story of the USS *Flier* has all the elements of a classic World War II survival tale: sudden disaster, physical deprivation, a ruthless enemy, friendly guerrillas, and an intricate escape. The eight men of the *Flier* became the first Americans of the Pacific war to survive the sinking of a submarine and make it back to the United States. It was rare for anyone from a lost submarine to ever be heard from again. Most often, submarines went down with all hands, and there was usually scant information about their last hours or days. The exceptions were the four submarines (*S-36, S-27, S-39,* and *Darter*) destroyed after running aground; in each case the entire crew was rescued. With the loss of fifty-two submarines and the death of more than 3,500 crewmen, the submarine service had the highest casualty rate of any branch of the U.S. military. There were known survivors from only eight

1

submarines sunk during the Pacific war, and apart from the eight men of the *Flier*, all these survivors spent the remainder of the war in Japanese captivity.

At the end of the war, Tom Paine of the USS *Pompon* was one of the officers who assisted in repatriating these submariners from Japanese prisoner of war camps. As the men passed through the American base at Guam, Paine was appalled by both their pitiful condition and their small number. Among his class at the Naval Academy, thirty-five men had volunteered for service on submarines, and seven of them had been lost at sea. The death rate was about the same throughout the submarine service. Paine had been best man at the wedding of one of those lost with the USS *Herring*, and he had been introduced to his future wife, a member of the Women's Auxiliary Australian Air Force in Perth, by a former Annapolis classmate lost with the USS *Lagarto*.[1]

The *Flier*'s skipper, John Daniel Crowley, was among the handful of men who escaped the sinking submarine and evaded capture in enemy territory. He also survived a naval judicial system notorious for its ruthlessness—twice. Earlier, the *Flier* had suffered a serious mishap on its first war patrol when it ran aground at Midway, resulting in the death of one crew member. Following a detailed inquiry into the incident, Crowley retained his command. After an extended period of repair, the *Flier* resumed its patrol, sailing from Pearl Harbor to the submarine base at Fremantle, Western Australia. The *Flier* was still in the early part of its second war patrol when it sank in Balabac Strait, this time leaving most of the crew on "eternal patrol," as the sailors put it. Despite a second formal inquiry after the *Flier*'s loss, Crowley would later be given another submarine command.

The naval inquiries, along with the *Flier*'s checkered history, open a rare window on the inner workings of the wartime "silent service." After the attack on Pearl Harbor, submarines became the first branch of the military to carry the fight to the enemy's doorstep. Although the major battles of the Pacific war were fought by aircraft carriers, U.S. submarines strangled the Japanese supply lines. Submariners represented less than 2 percent of U.S. Navy personnel, but they were responsible for more than half of Japan's shipping losses. In 1944 alone, U.S. subs sank nearly 500 Japanese ships, totaling well over 2 million tons.[2] This effectiveness was due in part to the fact that the activities of the submarine service were closely guarded secrets.

Although some of the *Flier*'s mysteries remain hidden beneath the sea, its fate reveals the vagaries of both underwater warfare and naval protocols. At one level, the *Flier*'s story suggests a high degree of cooperation among submariners, coast watchers, and guerrillas in the Philippines. At another level, it illustrates the infighting and personality clashes within the submarine command. The ordeal of the *Flier*'s crew and their loved ones also highlights the trauma and personal tragedies of the Pacific war, which were often obscured by acts of heroism.

1

The Aleutians

Lieutenant Commander John Daniel Crowley had paid his dues. Before being given command of the newly minted USS *Flier,* he had spent nearly two years in charge of an antiquated S-boat, popularly known in the navy as a "pigboat" or "sewer pipe." Conditions on the S-boats were atrocious. There were no showers on board and only one head for nearly fifty crewmen. Without air-conditioning, the boats accumulated an incredible stench during prolonged dives. Once the submarines surfaced, the sudden burst of oxygen could render the crew giddy. Even so, the sailors who served on S-boats took a certain pride in having the grit to withstand such discomfort for extended periods. As one writer put it, "An S-boat was a great leveling agent; all suffered equally."[1] To add to Crowley's suffering, he was assigned to some of the most inhospitable waters in the world.

Born in Springfield, Massachusetts, on 24 September 1908, John Crowley attended local schools before entering the U.S. Naval Academy in 1927. A classmate described Crowley's passage through the academy as "fairly easy sailing," and he loved sports.[2] When he graduated four years later, commissioned an ensign, Crowley became part of a group renowned for its social as well as military exclusivity. Nevertheless, it was a career characterized by relatively low pay and slow advancement. Like most new graduates, Crowley served on a succession of ships, including the battleships *Maryland* and *Arkansas* and the cruiser *Minneapolis*. On 25 June 1934 he was commissioned a lieutenant junior grade, and two years later he began instruction at the Submarine School in New London, Connecticut. It is possible that Crowley, like many other naval officers, viewed the submarine service as a shortcut to early command. After a period of postgraduate study at Annapolis and service on more surface ships and submarines, that ambition was finally realized.[3]

On 26 July 1941 Crowley assumed command of the *S-28*, built by the Bethlehem Shipbuilding Company at Quincy, Massachusetts. At the time, the *S-28* was nearly twenty years old and was one of twenty-six S-boats still in operation. As a lieutenant with some ten years' experience, Crowley was typical of the men given command of such boats.[4]

When the Japanese attacked Pearl Harbor in December 1941, the *S-28* was undergoing a much-needed overhaul at the Mare Island Naval Yard north of San Francisco. After the work was completed on 22 January 1942, the *S-28* headed for the Underwater Sound Training School at San Diego. Several months later the *S-28* was ordered to the less salubrious latitudes of the Aleutians, and it left San Diego on 20 May in the company of three other S-boats, headed for the American base at Dutch Harbor in Unalaska Bay.

The *S-28*'s deployment was in response to an anticipated Japanese attack on U.S. bases at Midway and in the Aleutians. The Aleutian Islands, extending southwest from Alaska in a forbidding necklace of rocks and shoals, became American territory when the United States purchased Alaska from the Russians in 1867. The ultimate Japanese strategy was to occupy the Aleutians and thus block an Allied advance in the northern Pacific and prevent the islands from being used as a base for long-range bombers. The more immediate objective was to create a diversion from a planned attack on Midway, an island group in the central Pacific. The Americans were well aware of the Japanese plans, however. A signals intelligence team at Pearl Harbor under Commander Joseph J. Rochefort had managed to crack the Japanese Fleet's general-purpose code used to transmit operational orders.[5]

Even with this knowledge, service in the Aleutians proved to be frustrating. Because of the anticipated Japanese strike, the S-boats were diverted from their original destination at Dutch Harbor and ordered into attack mode. On 2 June the *S-28* received a directive to attack enemy forces approaching Cold Bay on the Alaska Peninsula, but it was unable to make contact. The following day a Japanese task force under Vice Admiral Hosogaya unleashed its carrier aircraft on the American base at Dutch Harbor; more than a dozen fighters strafed the harbor and shore, followed by bombers.[6] Several days later, on 6–7 June, Japanese landing parties took possession of Attu and Kiska at the western end of the Aleutian chain. Although these islands were barely populated, they constituted additional losses for the Allies, who had already seen the fall of Singapore, Hong Kong, and the Philippines.

Still making their first patrol, Crowley and his crew encountered a Japanese destroyer on 18 June 1942 off the twenty-two-mile-long island of Kiska. They had been searching that morning in heavy seas for a tanker reported to be sailing from Attu to Kiska but had not encountered it. Near noon, however, through the patchy fog, they spotted a destroyer about a thousand yards away. The destroyer apparently detected the submarine minutes later and charged toward it. The *S-28* optimistically fired two torpedoes, using the destroyer's sound bearing, but the Japanese ship escaped unscathed and pursued the *S-28* for the next eight hours. This would be one of the few attacks made by the *S-28* under Crowley's command. He later described the remaining four patrols in the Aleutians as "principally reconnaissance patrols and notably lacking in targets."[7]

After the Battle of Midway, eight of the newer fleet submarines moved north and proved more successful against the enemy than the aging S-boats had been. The USS *Triton* sank a Japanese destroyer, the *Nenohi*, on 4 July 1942. The following day the USS *Growler* caught three destroyers at anchor, sinking one and severely damaging the others. The USS *Grunion,* making its first war

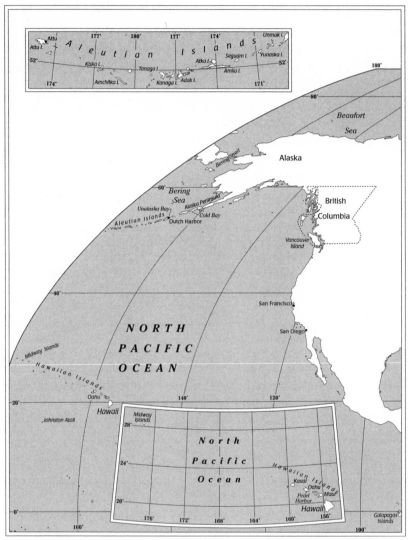

The Aleutian Islands and Midway

patrol, sank two Japanese submarine chasers on 15 July but then disappeared while patrolling in close proximity to the *S-28*. Crowley reportedly heard no depth charges or explosions to explain the *Grunion*'s loss—a stark reminder of the fragility of life on a submarine even without an attacking enemy.[8]

Crowley's main battles on the *S-28* were against the weather and the mechanical deficiencies of his submarine. The Aleutian Islands, strung out like vertebrae between the northern Pacific Ocean and the Bering Sea, are infamous for their extreme weather. Crowley and his crew faced a daily round of freezing temperatures, raging storms, gale-force winds, and impenetrable fogs. On the submarine's bridge, icy winds could freeze a man's hands to his binoculars. Inside, the dank environment of the S-boat after forty days on patrol was a hazard in itself. Condensation—so-called hull sweating—saturated the crew's bedding along with everything else. On his first patrol Crowley noted that the "air was always cold and damp."[9] To conserve battery power, they rarely turned on the heaters.

Because of the prolonged daylight hours in the northern latitudes, the *S-28* remained submerged an average of eighteen hours a day. Such lengthy dives wreaked havoc with the air quality inside the hull. Once carbon dioxide levels reached 3 percent, the atmosphere posed a serious threat to the crew, but even at lower levels it could cause headaches and other side effects.[10] The main methods of countering high carbon dioxide levels were to bleed stored oxygen into the submarine or to distribute carbon dioxide absorbent, but the *S-28* faced shortages of both.

The relatively brief periods on the surface also meant that the availability of fresh water was severely limited. Apart from what could be carried in storage tanks, the submarine's water supply depended on evaporators that ran off the heat of the diesel engine exhaust—and the *S-28* used diesel power only when it was on the surface (running on battery power when underwater). Besides the shortage of drinking water, what little water the crew did have was apparently tainted, causing many of the men to suffer from nausea and headaches. In addition, an outbreak of scabies, a contagious skin disease caused by parasitic mites, affected about a third of the men and was almost certainly exacerbated by the system of "hot bunking," in which crewmen shared the same beds as they rotated watches. To cap it off, there was a fire in the main port motor during the first patrol.

The *S-28* departed from Dutch Harbor for its second war patrol on 15 July 1942. Milder weather meant that the crew's health improved, and shorter daylight hours meant that they could spend more time on the surface. The submarine was stationed in the area off Kiska and received a number of directives to intercept enemy ships. Although some enemy contacts were made, the submarine never undertook an attack. The physical condition of the *S-28* remained a constant drawback. Among other things, the periscopes tended to fog up due to the differential between the water and air temperatures.[11]

The *S-28*'s third war patrol proved equally disappointing in terms of results, with only one enemy contact. In the late afternoon of 4 October 1942 the *S-28* sighted an enemy patrol vessel estimated to be 130 to 150 feet long. The submarine lost the initiative, however, and failed to make an attack. In fact, the only torpedo fired was launched by accident when a firing circuit malfunctioned.[12]

Throughout its three patrols, the *S-28*, like most S-boats, was handicapped by a lack of navigational equipment. Without radar, a Fathometer, or proper sound equipment, navigation was dangerous. Naval historian Samuel Eliot Morison once claimed that "navigating an S-boat was accomplished more by smell and feel than through science."[13] During the war, S-boats became notorious for running aground. For instance, on 20 January 1942 the *S-36* struck Taka Bakang Reef in Makassar Strait. With coral penetrating the hull, the submarine had to be abandoned. The crew was picked up by a Dutch merchantman and transported to Surabaya, Java. On 14 August 1942 the *S-39*, sailing out of Brisbane, Australia, ran aground in the Louisiade Archipelago off New Guinea. Again, the crew was lucky to survive, being rescued this time by the Australian corvette HMAS *Katoomba*.[14]

The navigational hazards in the Aleutians were potentially as lethal as those in the South Pacific. The often overcast conditions provided little opportunity to take visual bearings to determine a submarine's position, and unpredictable currents could sweep a craft far off course. Pinnacles of rock dotted the harbors and waters off the coast, and the presence of magnetic ores affected compass needles. Added to this was the inaccuracy of many of the charts supplied; on some maps, islands might be as much as five miles out of position, and there was no indication of depth soundings for many areas.[15]

While carrying out reconnaissance off Amchitka Island in June 1942, the S-27 was swept onto rocks 400 yards from the coast. Fortunately, all forty-nine crewmen were able to reach shore safely. Even the Japanese were not immune to the weather conditions: the Japanese submarine I-157 ran aground in the perpetual fog and was able to extricate itself only after firing all its torpedoes and throwing overboard a large number of the battery cells needed for underwater propulsion.[16]

After its third war patrol, the S-28 left Dutch Harbor and arrived in San Diego on 23 October 1942 to undergo dry-dock maintenance and the installation of some additional equipment, including the newly developed SJ radar system. This surface-searching radar, which sent out a rotating directional beam, would allow the submarine to track targets in the dark or in the poor visibility so prevalent in the Aleutians. It could detect a large ship 7,000 yards away and land up to 20,000 yards away. The S-28 would thus be able to contact a greater number of enemy ships, but the downside was that the new radar equipment required a lot of the S-28's scarcest resource—space—taking up a large part of the conning tower area and necessitating the removal of several crew bunks.[17] The S-28 also received a Fathometer, permitting accurate depth soundings, and a new Kleinschmidt distilling unit. The Kleinschmidt vapor-compression still could produce 750 gallons of fresh water a day, suitable for drinking as well as for use in storage batteries. Some considered the Kleinschmidt still one of the most important technical innovations of the submarine war.[18]

Departing San Diego on 9 December 1942, the S-28 commenced its fourth war patrol, terminating at Dutch Harbor on 21 January 1943. With the aid of radar, the submarine was able to make six enemy contacts, all during the hours of darkness. On two occasions the S-28 fired multiple torpedoes at targets but scored no hits. In what was becoming a recurring pattern, the patrol report endorsement by Crowley's superior officer read: "It is regretted that the USS *S-28* was unable to complete its attacks with success."[19]

During the *S-28*'s fifth war patrol in February 1943, the weather continued to be a major concern. Before going topside to man the bridge, crewmen had to dress in multiple layers of woolen underwear, shirts, sweaters, trousers, and socks. Crowley noted in his patrol report that the rubber-lined trousers and hooded jackets distributed to the crew generally provided good protection against the cold. Gloves, however, quickly filled with water, and whenever the men raised their arms, the icy liquid would pour down inside their jacket sleeves.[20] This time an endorsement described the patrol as "well conducted," even though the *S-28* had carried out no attacks and on 18 February had been bombed by a Japanese floatplane. In the grim conditions of the Aleutians, simply making it back constituted a successful mission.

Crowley was replaced as skipper of the *S-28* on 20 March 1943. The change of command took place at the Canadian naval base at Esquimalt, British Columbia, on the southern tip of Vancouver Island. The Canadian Pacific Fleet, lacking any submarines of its own, borrowed the *S-28* to practice antisubmarine training.[21] The *S-28*'s new skipper, Vincent A. Sisler, had seen action with the fleet submarine *Sailfish,* and although he had experienced defective torpedoes and depth charge attacks, Sisler considered the southwestern Pacific a place for "sissies" compared with conditions in the Aleutians.[22]

In May 1943 the Americans would retake Attu from the Japanese after a bitter fight. Under the command of Rear Admiral Thomas C. Kinkaid, the Americans made their third amphibious landing assault of the war on the south coast of the island at the aptly named Massacre Bay (Russian Cossacks had slaughtered Aleuts at the site two centuries earlier). The submarines *Narwhal* and *Nautilus* played a role in U.S. operations, slipping in 200 army scouts before the main landing. Although the battle for Attu was expected to last three days, it continued for three weeks, with heavy casualties from both the fighting and the cruel weather. In the soggy tundra, the Americans' military vehicles proved largely useless, and many of the troops contracted trench foot. Nevertheless, of the 2,000 Japanese defending the island, fewer than 30 survived to become prisoners of war.[23]

Having captured Attu, the Americans turned their attention to the Japanese fortifications on the bat-shaped island of Kiska. On 15 August 1943, after a prolonged bombardment, almost 35,000 U.S. troops staged another amphibious landing on Kiska's rocky beaches. They were surprised to find the island deserted; the Japanese garrison had slipped away in the murky mists. Admiral Kinkaid described the action as "a darn good dress rehearsal under combat conditions really."[24] Even so, the Americans suffered several hundred casualties, largely from "friendly fire" by jittery troops in the fog.

The *S-28* made two more war patrols in northern latitudes before heading for the friendlier climate of Pearl Harbor, where it arrived on 16 November 1943. After an overhaul, the aging submarine was utilized for training exercises. By the end of 1943, all the S-boats had been relegated to training or less active patrol duties.[25]

Despite being taken out of combat and assigned to the warmer waters of Hawaii, a grim fate awaited the *S-28*. Naval reservist Jack G. Campbell assumed command of the *S-28* on 20 June 1944. On 4 July, while participating in sonar exercises with the Coast Guard cutter *Reliance,* the submarine vanished. When the *Reliance* lost contact with the *S-28*, it summoned additional ships from Pearl Harbor to join the search, but they found only a large oil slick where the submarine had last dived. In waters more than 8,000 feet deep, rescue or salvage was not a possibility. A subsequent inquiry concluded that the submarine had probably lost depth control, but there was no way of knowing whether this had resulted from mechanical failure or human error. Less than two months later, John Crowley's next command, the USS *Flier,* would be lost as well.

2

A New Boat

John Crowley's reward for his perseverance with the *S-28* was command of the brand-new fleet submarine the USS *Flier* (SS-250). After being replaced on the *S-28* in March 1943, Crowley attended the Prospective Commanding Officer School at New London, Connecticut. All officers receiving their first command or a newly constructed ship were required to take a four-week course of lectures and practical training. With its focus on attack techniques and rigorous exercises at sea, the course would later be called the "Command Class in Attack Technique."[1]

Beginning in July 1943 Crowley was involved in fitting out the *Flier* at Groton, Connecticut. The *Flier*'s keel had been laid at the Electric Boat Company in Groton many months earlier, on 30 October 1942. Originally known as the Electric Storage Battery Company, Electric Boat had obtained patents in 1897 for the first submarine capable of recharging its own batteries while at sea. From that point on, Electric Boat built the lion's share of the U.S. Navy's submarines.

The U.S. submarine-building program first picked up during World War I and continued to gain momentum thereafter. Following the fall of France in May 1940, Congress approved the building of more than seventy new submarines. By July 1941 Electric Boat had eleven ways in operation for submarine construction. By March 1943 an additional ten ways were in use at a new facility called the Victory Yard. The USS *Dace* (SS-247) became the first submarine built at the Victory Yard, as production reached full throttle. With the motto "Keep 'em sliding," swing shifts operated twenty-four hours a day. By the time the *Flier* was launched in July 1943, a new submarine was being completed at Electric Boat every other week.[2]

The official launching of ships served a number of purposes beyond simply carrying on a naval tradition. At times, the launching of a new craft reflected the family networks so pervasive in the navy. For instance, when Slade Cutter was assigned to the newly constructed USS *Requin,* his wife became the sponsor and officially christened the submarine on 1 January 1945. At other times, ship launchings provided an occasion to grease the wheels of bureaucracy and consolidate government patronage. Thus, when the USS *Missouri* was launched, Senator Harry S. Truman of Missouri was the principal speaker at the event, and Truman's daughter, Margaret, christened the ship. The ceremony would prove prophetic: when Japan surrendered, Truman was president of the United States, and it was Truman who decided that the surrender ceremony at Tokyo Bay should be carried out on the deck of the *Missouri.*[3]

With less spectacular results, the launch of the USS *Flier* was similarly politicized. The secretary of the navy designated Mrs. Anna Smith Pierce from Lynchburg, South Carolina, the *Flier*'s sponsor. Not coincidentally, she was the daughter of Ellison DuRant Smith, a member of the Senate's Naval Affairs Committee. Smith had first been elected to the Senate as a South Carolina Democrat in 1908. He gained the nickname "Cotton Ed" for his efforts on behalf of the Southern Cotton Association. Any anticipated gains from Smith's navy patronage proved short-lived, however. He died on 17 November 1944, barely a year after the *Flier* was commissioned.

The launch of the *Flier* was, as expected, organized with military precision, and press releases were distributed to the South Carolina newspapers. Mrs. Pierce, along with her sister-in-law Mrs. Farley Smith, would depart South Carolina by train on 9 July

1943. They were scheduled to arrive at Groton on Sunday, 11 July, at 3:30 P.M., with the ceremony set to commence at 4:45 P.M. The two women would begin their return trip the same evening.

Employees of Electric Boat, along with their families, were encouraged to attend the launch ceremony at the company's Victory Yard. To reduce worker absenteeism, the ceremony included a raffle in which maintenance electricians with perfect attendance records would have the chance to win a $25 war bond.[4]

Veteran skipper Glynn R. "Donc" Donaho delivered the keynote address at the *Flier*'s launch. Lieutenant Commander Donaho, then on leave, had been recommended by Commander Lewis Parks to give the approximately five-minute speech. Donaho had been awarded three Navy Crosses, the navy's second highest combat decoration. He had a reputation as a "spit and polish guy" who was a stickler for military protocol. Paul Schratz, who encountered Donaho at New London, described him as "humorless and a rigid perfectionist."[5] Donaho's notorious inflexibility had been demonstrated in 1942 as he commanded the *Flying Fish* on its maiden cruise from New London to Pearl Harbor. Despite spotting a Nazi U-boat on the way to Panama, he made no attempt to close with the enemy, stating that his operation orders said nothing about attacking enemy ships while in transit. As a result, all future operation orders were altered to specifically direct an attack on any enemy craft encountered. For the *Flier*'s launch, Donaho chose as his text, "Building Subs that Can 'Take It' in Battle." Electric Boat's personnel manager, A. D. Barnes, later assured Donaho that his talk had been "one of the finest that we have had in the plant thus far" and claimed that it would inspire "increased efforts to build better submarines."[6]

Apart from Crowley, there were a number of other submarine commanders and their wives in attendance at the *Flier*'s launch ceremony. Some of these men had already gained outstanding reputations, such as Reuben Whitaker and William Stovall. Also present was Admiral Freeland A. Daubin, commander of submarines in the Atlantic.[7] (Daubin would later assume an important, if unexpected, role following the loss of the *Flier* in 1944.) At precisely 5:00 P.M. the *Flier*'s hull slid stern-first down the Victory Yard's way number five into the Thames River. For many of those present, these moments were full of pride and anticipation. Later the hull would be towed a few miles upstream to Electric Boat's fitting-out basin, and the submarine would be completed over the next three months.

As the *Flier*'s prospective commanding officer, Crowley's job was to serve as both observer and adviser in the final stages of construction. He had access to the blueprints (covering a quarter of an acre), as well as other machinery and equipment specifications. It was his right to suggest modifications or to complain if he found any workmanship deficient.[8] The fitting-out period allowed the officers and some key enlisted men to begin familiarizing themselves with their new submarine. They also had the opportunity to attend special schools covering such subjects as gunnery, sonar, and mine warfare. Most important, this time allowed the men to begin bonding with one another and forging a cohesive fighting unit. On 18 October 1943 the *Flier* was officially commissioned under Crowley's command.

As a fleet boat, the *Flier* (named after a common species of sunfish) offered a stark contrast to the old S-boats. The first of the larger and more agile fleet boats had begun appearing in 1933, and about forty were in service at the start of World War II. The *Flier* was almost a third longer than the *S-28* and could carry nearly twice the crew. With a greater periscope depth, fleet boats were less likely to be rammed by enemy ships. Whereas the old S-boats had riveted hulls, the *Flier* was constructed with welded seams, a method first introduced in the early 1930s. Welded hulls were stronger and could be made from lighter materials. Welded hulls were also cheaper to build, requiring less skilled labor and no plate overlap. Most important, there were no rivets to pop out in the likely event of a depth charge attack.[9]

The *Flier* had ten torpedo tubes, compared with only four on the *S-28*. Equipped with the latest in radar, the submarine could detect ships 20,000 yards away. When used in combination with the plan position indicator, the radar system provided a two-dimensional image of surface targets in relation to the submarine. At the same time, the torpedo data computer on board allowed more sophisticated attacks. On the S-boats, angles of fire had to be preset by hand, and the submarine needed to be more or less pointed in the direction of the torpedo track. On fleet boats, in contrast, the torpedo data computer automatically adjusted gyro angles on the torpedoes and offered the best submarine fire-control system in the world.[10]

Before departing for a forward base, all new submarines went through a shakedown period of testing. Originally the shakedown period was six weeks, but starting in July 1943 it was reduced to thirty days. The crew then underwent two more weeks of training at Pearl Harbor. With a critical need for manpower, some crew had little preparation for submarine duty. Although young officers were occasionally sent straight to new constructions, most officers attended the Submarine School at New London. There, they spent their mornings in classes and their afternoons working in an attack or diving trainer. Some of those with technical aptitude spent their time at New London studying radar exclusively. Others were given specialized training at universities, such as electrical engineering at Texas A&M. Regardless of his background, every officer would eventually be required to go before a qualification board.[11]

Once on board a submarine, the officers and petty officers began the process of qualifying the men under their command in what was known as the "School of the Boat." Each man had an assigned station, but all crew members were expected to have a grasp of the equipment throughout the submarine. It was an arduous process that involved both studying plans and gaining practical experience in each compartment until the men knew the function of every pipe, valve, and piece of machinery. Eventually, when the chief of the boat deemed a sailor ready, he would undergo both an oral and a practical examination given by the officers.[12]

The *Flier* sailed from New London for Pearl Harbor on 20 December 1943. As the submarine approached Panama in the Caribbean

Sea, it was attacked by a "friendly" merchant ship. The merchant-man fired off thirteen shells before the *Flier* managed to disappear, still on the surface, into a rain squall.

Despite designated safety zones and recognition signals, such attacks were unnervingly common. The *Flier*'s executive officer, Lieutenant James Liddell, had already experienced a "friendly" attack while serving on the USS *Snapper*. As that submarine had traversed the Indian Ocean on its way to a patrol in the Philippines, an amphibious patrol bomber had dropped two bombs nearby. Liddell later described the damage to the *Snapper* as "fairly limited."[13]

Like the *Flier*, a number of new submarines received their baptism of fire from Allied ships and aircraft while making their way from New London to Pearl Harbor. The USS *Scorpion* was fired on by a merchant ship as it cruised between Panama and Hawaii. The USS *Harder* was strafed and bombed by an American patrol plane as it made its way through the Caribbean a week after departing New London. The USS *Dorado*, similarly en route to Panama, was sunk by an American aircraft only six days before the *Flier* was commissioned. News of the *Dorado*'s loss with all hands naturally upset the *Flier*'s green crew.[14]

3

Midway

War manufactures death and irony in abundance, as the men of the *Flier* would discover only days into their first war patrol. Although John Crowley had managed to evade the myriad hazards of the Aleutian Islands for five patrols in the antiquated *S-28*, he would come to grief in his brand-new submarine on its first outing in the Pacific. The *Flier* departed Pearl Harbor at 1:23 P.M. on 12 January 1944, and only four days later it would be a wreck at Midway.

The circular atoll known as Midway lies some 1,250 miles from Pearl Harbor, about one-third the distance from Hawaii to Tokyo. Surrounded by a ring of coral reef five miles in diameter are a number of tiny plots of dry land. The largest island of the group, Sand Island, is only a mile and a half long by half a mile wide. The next largest island, Eastern Island, is a mile and a quarter long and three-quarters of a mile wide. This rather pathetic piece of real estate would assume enormous importance in the Pacific war.

Back in July 1859, N. B. Brooks, captain of the Honolulu-based ship *Gambia,* laid claim to the atoll for the United States under the Guano Islands Act of 1856. The Guano Act enabled U.S. citizens to temporarily occupy unclaimed Pacific islands in order to harvest the bird droppings for fertilizer. Brooks called the place Middlebrooks, partly in an attempt at self-aggrandizement, and

21

partly in recognition of its location between Japan and the west coast of the United States.

Less than a decade later, in August 1867, Captain William Reynolds took formal possession of the Midway islands for the United States, under instructions from the secretary of the navy. There was little interest in the atoll until the turn of the century, when a transpacific cable was laid. In 1900 the tugboat *Iroquois* was dispatched to take soundings at Midway, and the crew discovered Japanese killing the local birds for their plumage. A series of protests by the U.S. government against Japanese poachers and squatters followed, and President Theodore Roosevelt placed Midway under the authority of the Department of the Navy on 20 January 1903.

Midway next became a cable station and received something of a makeover. Daniel Morrison, the station's superintendent from 1906 to 1921, imported grass, shrubs, and casuarina trees to be planted on the aptly named Sand Island. In August 1921 the tanker *Patoka* arrived to service U.S. Navy ships in the area. In 1935 Midway also became a refueling stop for Pan American Airlines, and Pan Am built a small, low-lying hotel at the northeastern end of Sand Island.

With the approach of war, Midway was proclaimed a national defense area under an executive order dated 14 February 1941. The U.S. Navy had already completed a barracks on Sand Island in 1940, and there was additional construction of hangars, fuel tanks, water towers, and a 5,300-foot runway on triangular Eastern Island.[1]

On the same day as the attack on Pearl Harbor, 7 December 1941, Japanese destroyers shelled Midway as both a diversion and a preemptive strike to protect the returning Japanese fleet. The next month, three Japanese submarines lobbed some shells at Midway as they passed by. They got off only a few rounds before return fire from shore batteries convinced them to dive.

Midway would assume center stage in June 1942. The Japanese hoped to seize the islands and establish a forward air base there. Under the plan devised by Admiral Isoruku Yamamoto, after softening up American defenses with bombardment by Japanese aircraft, a dozen troopships would land an occupation force of 5,000 men. Possession of Midway would extend Japan's lines of defense some 2,000 miles east. With a base there, Japanese planes and ships could threaten the American west coast and disrupt supply lines to the southwestern Pacific. The main objective of the attack, however, was to lure the U.S. carrier fleet from Pearl Harbor into a "decisive battle" and destroy it.[2]

By mid-May, Admiral Chester Nimitz already knew that the Japanese were planning an attack on Midway, along with an invasion of the Aleutian Islands (which led to Crowley and the *S-28* being sent to Alaskan waters). In what some view as the Allied code breakers' greatest triumph, they were able to discern the Japanese stratagem. The main U.S. submarine force was therefore deployed in a defensive perimeter around Midway. By 3 June, a total of twenty-five submarines, mainly en route to patrols, were stationed at the approaches to the atoll.[3]

When the Battle of Midway erupted on 4 June 1942, submarines played a minor role in what was primarily a contest between aircraft carriers. Fortunately for the Americans, the Japanese advance force of submarines, sent to scout Midway, arrived too late. By the time the submarines were on station, the U.S. carriers had already crossed their patrol lines. U.S. submarines, in contrast, did influence the course of events. The USS *Nautilus* was the only submarine to launch an attack on the Japanese fleet, and even though its torpedoes missed their mark, the Japanese left the destroyer *Arashi* behind to mount a depth charge attack on the upstart submarine. When the *Arashi* later headed north to catch up with the rest of the fleet, the Japanese position was given away when the destroyer was spotted by U.S. aircraft. Planes from the USS *Enterprise* subsequently bombed the heavy carriers *Akagi* and *Kaga*. The Japanese ships were caught with refueled planes on their decks, which added to the damage and forced the ships out of the battle.

Similarly, the USS *Tambor* contributed indirectly to the Americans' success. In the early hours of 5 June, a group of four Japanese cruisers spotted the submarine, and in their haste to evade a possible attack, the *Mogami* rammed the *Mikuma*. The damaged Japanese ships then made relatively easy targets for U.S. aircraft, which further damaged the *Mogami* and sank the *Mikuma*. More generally, various submarine sightings distracted Admiral Osami Nagumo, causing him to send out short-range antisubmarine patrols rather than long-range scouts searching for the U.S. carrier fleet.[4]

The Battle of Midway would later be described as a turning point of the war, and some deemed it the decisive naval confrontation in the Pacific. With the destruction of four of its aircraft carriers and a thousand planes, Japan lost both its naval airpower superiority and its psychological edge in orchestrating the war. Many of the Japanese pilots who had participated in the attack on Pearl Harbor six months earlier were killed and would prove to be largely irreplaceable. In Japan, accounts of the defeat were suppressed; the surviving crews were even denied shore leave, lest they spread the demoralization. Although the United States lost the carrier *Yorktown* and more than a hundred aircraft, its industrial strength meant that Japan could never regain naval superiority. Admiral Ernest King lauded the battle as "the first decisive defeat suffered by the Japanese Navy in 350 years."[5]

Whether any of the *Flier*'s crew members were reflecting on these dramatic events as they approached Midway is uncertain. For most of the men it was simply a pit stop on the way to the real action. Charles Lockwood, commander of submarines in the Pacific, had fought hard to establish Midway as a submarine base, eventually persuading Admiral Nimitz to divert the necessary dredging equipment and other resources. Given that Midway was nearly 1,300 miles closer to Japan than Pearl Harbor was, topping up fuel tanks there could considerably extend the range and length of a patrol.[6]

The amenities on Midway remained spartan. When the USS *Gurnard* moored at Midway on 17 April 1943, crewman Bill Gleason wrote in his diary, "This place is a mess, nothing but sand

and more sand."⁷ Although it had been developed as a leave center, submariners were far less enthusiastic about spending their precious time at Midway than at Pearl Harbor or at Fremantle, Australia. When the crew of the *Pollack* was forced to take leave at Midway in April 1943, they were disgusted to find "no girls, no hard liquor, no nightlife, and no entertainment."⁸ The main attractions were the beaches, along with tubs of ice-cold beer, poker games, and good food. Another favorite pastime of the submarine crews at Midway was to watch the peculiar antics of the local Laysan albatross—or gooney birds—well known for their mating dances and incompetent landings. Unfortunately, the birds had to be continually chased off the volleyball courts, and their noise tended to keep crews awake at night.⁹

The *Flier* established radar contact with Midway at half past noon on 16 January 1944. Even before it was sighted, the atoll's presence was usually obvious by the hundreds of birds wheeling overhead—terns, gulls, and pelicans, as well as gooneys. By 1:15 P.M. Midway's low islands could be made out (the highest point on Sand Island was forty-three feet). At 2:00 P.M. the *Flier* was just south of the entrance buoys to Midway Channel. An anchor detail was already waiting on the after 20 mm gun platform.

The first attempts to deepen the harbor at Midway had taken place in 1870. A wall of coral some 6 to 15 feet wide circled the lagoon, and in 1923 a hole had been blasted in the southern reef to run the transpacific cable. In 1938 the U.S. Navy had begun to dredge a channel between Sand Island and Eastern Island. When the *Flier* arrived at Midway, the channel was less than 40 feet deep and measured 400 feet wide at its narrowest point.¹⁰

Weather-wise, it was not a good day at Midway. Although the atoll was situated only several hundred miles north of the Hawaiian Islands, the winter weather could be severe. In between sunny days, cold gales could whip the lagoon into a choppy mass of whitecaps. As the *Flier* sat off the entrance buoys, squalls of rain passed over, at times totally obscuring the islands. Rough seas shuddered against the submarine from the southwest, with some waves exceeding twenty feet. Because of the high seas and big waves, Crowley ordered a change from diesel power to battery power. On diesel power, there was a danger of waves swamping the boat through the main induction. On battery power, with the main induction closed, the *Flier* was less vulnerable to suddenly being pooped by high swells. As another concession to the rough weather, the anchor party was stationed on the gun platform instead of on the more exposed deck.[11]

At 2:15 P.M. the *Flier* exchanged signals with a tower on Sand Island. The submarine received instructions to stand by for a pilot. As the *Flier* waited, some of the crew remarked about the strength of the submarine's welding, joking that they hoped the hull would not break in half in the rough seas.[12]

4

Grounded

The *Flier*'s stopover at Midway, intended as a brief visit to refuel, turned into a weeklong ordeal. Waiting outside the Midway Channel, the *Flier* prepared to take a pilot on board from the tugboat *YT-188*. The tug pulled alongside the submarine's lee side, but the seas were too high to contemplate transferring personnel. Someone shouted through a megaphone from the *YT-188*, but he could not be heard over the roar of the wind and the ocean. The tug then signaled by semaphore for the *Flier* to follow it into the lagoon.[1]

At about 3:00 P.M., some half a mile south of the entrance buoys, the *Flier* began trailing the tug from a distance of about 750 yards. With Crowley conning the submarine, they proceeded at two-thirds speed, or ten knots. Crowley feared overtaking the tug if he ran at standard speed, which was fifteen knots. The *Flier* passed between the channel entrance buoys about twenty minutes later. In addition to Crowley, the men on the bridge included Lieutenant James Liddell, acting as officer of the deck. The chief quartermaster on the bridge was Albert Leightley; he communicated orders through a voice tube to the helmsman in the conning tower. Seaman First Class James D. Russo had been the helmsman since the *Flier*'s commissioning, but he had only a few months on the job. As they passed the entrance buoys, Leightley jumped down to the conning tower to check on Russo. Leightley had been to Midway before and knew from experience that steering in the chan-

27

nel could be tricky. The executive officer, Lieutenant Commander Benjamin Ernest Adams Jr., acted as navigator. The rain and sea spray made it too wet to use a chart, so Adams alternated between the bridge and the conning tower, where he checked navigational aids through the periscope. As the *Flier* entered the channel, a rain-squall reduced visibility, and Adams tried to take bearings through the periscope.

Just as it passed the entrance buoys, the submarine yawed suddenly to the left as it was hit by heavy swells. Part of the problem seemed to be the *Flier*'s reduced speed. Without enough momentum, the vessel was being lifted and thrown off course by the surf. An order was given to change course to the right, but then the submarine yawed sharply to the right. Lieutenant Liddell relayed an order to the helmsman for full left rudder; in the heavy seas, though, the vessel responded lethargically. As they swung to the left, the crew could feel the submarine hit bottom with a sickening shudder. Rising swells lifted the *Flier* momentarily before it slammed into the reef again. Crowley tried to maneuver the submarine to the west, and when the seas lifted the boat again, he ordered all ahead full. Again the submarine struck the bottom.

Belowdecks, Earl Baumgart had recently finished his watch in the engine room. He had cleaned up a bit and then went to lie on his bunk. Suddenly he found himself thrown on the deck with a number of other men. They knew immediately that they had either run aground or collided with something, and they headed toward the control room to find out what had happened. As they passed through the crew's mess, they found it in disarray, with pots, food, and drink strewn about.[2]

In the maneuvering room, the shock of the grounding knocked a large tool chest from its mounting, and a screwdriver flew from the chest into the main terminal of the number four motor. This caused a short circuit, which ignited a pile of rags in the corner of the motor room. The maneuvering room was soon filled with smoke, and the crew had to deal with a fire on top of their other worries.

Meanwhile, Crowley tried to use the propellers and rudder to winch the submarine free of the reef. In addition to the fire, there were now reports of flooding in the torpedo room and the motor room. The situation looked grim enough for Lieutenant Liddell to ask Crowley whether they should evacuate the men from belowdecks. Crowley replied, "Not yet," but he gave an order for all the men below to put on their life belts.[3]

Standing ready topside, the anchor detail was ordered forward. It was hoped that dropping anchor would prevent the *Flier* from being pulled back farther onto the reef. Members of the anchor party, stationed on the after 20 mm gun platform, were wearing rough-weather parkas and overalls, but they had no life belts, and this would have dire consequences.

Ensign Herbert Albert Baehr, nicknamed "Teddy," was acting as junior officer of the deck. He led the three-man anchor detail down the starboard ladder of the gun platform to the deck. Baehr was then ordered back to the platform, and a short time later he was sent to get a report on the fire in the maneuvering room. He found that the men below had managed to extinguish the fire in about ten minutes, which was good news. When Baehr returned to the bridge, however, he was told that there were men overboard.[4]

While Ensign Baehr was investigating the fire below, Crowley had ordered the anchor detail forward to stand by the anchor gear. Just as they reached the forward section of the conning tower, a massive wave broke over the deck. Waite Hoyt Daggy, fireman first class, managed to grab the doghouse door of the conning tower but suffered a bad gash on his chin. A short, muscular man from the state of Washington, Daggy would carry the scar for the rest of his life.[5] Kenneth Leroy Gwinn, chief torpedoman's mate, was also sent sprawling back into the conning tower. He managed to claw his way back to the bridge and the gun platform. The third man, James Cahl, last seen carrying an anchor wrench, was swept overboard.[6]

Lieutenant Liddell had initially been watching as the anchor detail moved forward on the forecastle, but his attention had been diverted elsewhere when he heard the cry, "Man overboard."

From his vantage point on the bridge, Crowley could see a man in the water about twenty yards off the port side, adjacent to the forward capstan. Another crewman, Joseph Antoine Lia, would later describe Cahl as having "a hopeless look on his face" as he treaded water with his arms outstretched.[7]

There were, in fact, two men overboard. Clyde Gerber also ended up in the raging sea, about twenty yards off the submarine's port side, parallel to the four-inch deck gun. A life ring and three life belts were heaved into the ocean, but none of them landed close enough for either Cahl or Gerber to grab on to. Liddell called for a strong swimmer from among the men gathered on the gun platform. George Joseph Banchero, motor machinist's mate second class, came forward and stripped off his clothes. Wearing an inflated life belt and carrying a cork life ring, he went over the port side near the engine air induction. By this time, Gerber had drifted back more or less even with the conning tower. Cahl, however, had been swept about fifty yards off the bow and already looked beyond help. He could be glimpsed through the waves periodically, but soon after Banchero went into the water, Cahl disappeared from view entirely.

In the turbulent water, Banchero was soon stripped of the life ring, and he had difficulty spotting Gerber over the waves. From the conning tower, Liddell motioned both men to head for the beach rather than try to swim back to the *Flier*. Banchero finally reached Gerber, and the two men struck out toward Eastern Island. They spent the next three hours struggling in the water but were eventually discovered standing together on a sand spit.

Apparently on his own initiative, Joseph Lia, torpedoman's mate third class, also went into the water to try to assist his crewmates. Lia had initially been on deck as a line handler when the plan had been to dock with the pilot tug. Upon seeing the men in the water, he put on an inflated life belt, and Kenneth Gwinn from the anchor detail secured a line to him. Ensign Baehr tended the line as Lia jumped over the side and struck out toward Cahl and Gerber. He was unable to make any headway, though, and drifted back toward the stern of the submarine. Lia was hauled to safety and sent below to be checked out by the pharmacist's mate.

As these events unfolded, orders were given to lighten the submarine in the hope that it would float off the reef. Baehr was again ordered below to get a report on all variable ballast. Finding no one available to help him, Baehr blew overboard two of the fuel ballast tanks and two of the regular fuel tanks. He also pumped out all the variable ballast tanks inside the pressure hull, but the *Flier* still would not budge, and the current continued to drive the submarine east into shallow water.

At 3:45 P.M. normal steering was lost, and the helmsman had to shift to emergency steering by hand. The continual pounding of the rudder on the bottom, however, made it impossible to regain control. Fifteen minutes later the crew tried to release the anchor, but it was jammed. The packing glands around the propeller shafts were also leaking badly by this time, and water poured into the maneuvering room.

Suddenly, the hope of rescue appeared. The USS *Macaw* made its way toward the floundering submarine, anchored a short distance away, and signaled that it would try to pass the *Flier* a line.

5

USS *Macaw*

By 4:00 P.M. the USS *Macaw* (ASR-11) was anchored off the Midway entrance buoys. The plan was to float a line to the *Flier* and tow the submarine off the reef. Unfortunately, the *Macaw*'s next message stated starkly: "We are aground."[1] The *Macaw* had grounded less than 100 yards west of the submarine.

The 250-foot-long, 2,000-ton *Macaw* was a Chanticleer class submarine rescue vessel. Built in Oakland, California, the ship had been commissioned on 12 July 1942, making it about a year older than the *Flier*. The *Macaw* carried a complement of 102 crewmen, heavy-lifting machinery, and deep-sea diving equipment, including the McCann rescue chamber. The rescue bell, some ten feet high by seven feet wide, was designed to convey men from a sunken submarine to the surface. It would be of no use, however, in dealing with the *Flier*'s situation.[2]

The *Macaw*'s skipper, Paul Willis Burton, was well known within the fraternity of submariners. Beginning in 1929 the navy required the captains of rescue and salvage ships to have experience with both submarines and deep-sea diving. Burton had not only trained at the New London Submarine School but had also been the officer in charge of its underwater escape training tank. That 138-foot-high, silo-shaped tank near the Thames River was the most obvious landmark at New London, and the escape exercise was an ordeal that most submariners never forgot.

33

After first being tested in a decompression chamber, submariner candidates had to simulate a submarine escape using the Momsen lung, named for its creator Charles "Swede" Momsen. The apparatus, designed specifically to facilitate the escape from a submarine stranded beneath the surface, consisted of a black rubber bag with a nose clip and a mouthpiece. A canister of soda and lime filtered out carbon dioxide and, at least in theory, allowed the submariner to breathe as he slowly made his way to the surface. Momsen had experienced firsthand the horrible sensation of being stuck underwater. During his first command on the *O-15,* the bow planes had jammed during a dive, causing the submarine to burrow into the muddy bottom. The vessel managed to surface only after the crew blasted water out of the forward torpedo tubes.[3]

Momsen, acclaimed by some as America's greatest submariner, also had a hand in constructing the training tanks at New London. Submarine trainees descended 100 feet to the bottom of the water tank on a platform. Then, equipped with the Momsen lung, they had to slowly make their way to the top. Burton, known for his puckish sense of humor, had life-size pictures of curvaceous mermaids painted on the inner walls of the tank to mark various depths.[4]

Despite the experience of Burton and his crew, their efforts to rescue the *Flier* had ended in disaster. With the *Macaw* stranded and all hope of an immediate rescue abandoned, the *Flier's* crew tried to brace for what would be a long, uneasy night. Tanks were flooded to try to stabilize the submarine on the reef and reduce the pounding it was taking from the rough seas.

By Monday morning, 17 January, the seas were a bit calmer, but there was no plan to try to refloat the *Flier.* By late morning, after several unsuccessful attempts, the men managed to fix a line and a wire between the submarine and the *Macaw.* Both vessels rode out another night on the reef as the seas continued to moderate.[5]

On Tuesday morning the *Flier* began transferring some of its crew to the *Macaw* via a boatswain chair—a daunting experience. The boatswain chair, resembling a swing, was suspended from a line between the two ships and tended to sag perilously as the crafts rolled with the motion of the sea. Earl Baumgart was among those evacuated from the submarine, and he said a silent prayer as he began the transfer from the *Flier* to the *Macaw*. With both ships rocking, the boatswain chair hit the water at one point, and Baumgart inflated his life vest, fearing that the line might snap. Eventually, he made it safely to the *Macaw*.[6]

On Wednesday morning the weather took another turn for the worse. The wind picked up, and it began to rain heavily. The *Flier* flooded the number one main ballast tank to try to prevent further drifting of the stern. At 4:00 in the afternoon the submarine received a portable high-frequency radio from the *Macaw* to facilitate communications.

By Thursday morning, 20 January, the *Flier* had drifted farther onto the reef. But again, it appeared that salvation might be at hand. At 8:30 A.M. the submarine rescue vessel USS *Florikan* was spotted on the horizon. Under the command of George Sharp, the *Florikan* had made the trip from Pearl Harbor specifically to help rescue the *Flier* and tow it back to Pearl.

Later that morning, at about 10:30 A.M., the body of James Cahl washed up on the beach at Midway. The senior medical officer, Ivan F. Duff, and the senior dental officer, Clement T. Hughes, confirmed Cahl's identity from dental records. The following morning at 11:00 A.M., Cahl's body was committed to the deep in a Protestant burial ceremony conducted on a motor torpedo boat. Although the specific details of Cahl's burial are unknown, the rituals were highly standardized. The body was either sewn into a canvas shroud or placed in a weighted coffin. An honor platoon was typically assembled on deck, and a service of scripture and prayers was read by a chaplain or another officer. At the appointed time, six to eight pallbearers tilted a board holding the body, sliding it feetfirst from under the national ensign into the sea. A party of seven men then fired three volleys into the air, a custom originally supposed to drive away evil spirits. The playing of taps followed. Under the direction of a chief master-at-arms, the flag was then encased and delivered to the commanding officer.[7]

Most of Cahl's shipmates were still on the beleaguered submarine when he was buried at sea. Those who had already transferred to shore were not allowed to attend the ceremony, ostensibly to avoid the risk of any further loss of life in the rough conditions.[8] Later that day, Cahl's personal effects were transferred to the *Macaw* via boatswain chair. Crowley was faced with the grim task of writing to Cahl's family and explaining the circumstances of his loss. As it happened, Cahl was one of the relatively few enlisted men on the *Flier* who was married.

Cahl's crewmates likely found his death difficult to accept. In some ways, an accidental death was even more tragic than one that was combat related. The crew of the USS *Pollack,* for instance, was devastated when one of its members was crushed to death between two torpedoes while on patrol.[9] And Cahl would not be the last submariner to drown at Midway. Only a couple of months later, on 5 March, the body of George Hepfler from the USS *Archerfish* would be recovered from the lagoon. Like Cahl, the waters at Midway became his final resting place.[10]

On Saturday, 22 January, at about 8:00 A.M., Waite Daggy was finally transferred to the *Macaw* and then sent to the Midway base hospital for treatment of his injured chin.[11] A total of twenty-three men left the submarine and were shuttled to land. There, they learned that their crewmate Clyde Gerber, last seen standing on a sand spit, was in the hospital with a fractured left arm.

By that time, the *Flier* had been stuck on the reef for six days, being battered much of that time by heavy seas and waves that were sometimes high enough to break over the submarine's bridge. For Crowley it had been a painful and humiliating week, especially as he watched other submarines arrive en route to patrols. That Saturday morning, for example, the USS *Kingfish* made its way past the stranded *Flier* to the Midway harbor.

At a little after 9:00 in the morning the *Flier* received a towing bridle from the *Macaw,* which was rigged around the submarine's four-inch deck gun. At around noon the *Gaylord,* a floating steam crane used for construction work, was towed by two tugs within a couple hundred yards of the *Flier* off the channel entrance. The *Flier* crew later hauled aboard a towing bridle from the *Gaylord* and cast off all lines except for a two-inch-diameter wire from the crane. The anchor was then pulled in, and the submarine lightened. With the aid of the crane, the *Flier* finally floated free of the reef at 2:29 P.M. By 2:45 the *YT-188*, the tug originally intended to lead the *Flier* into the Midway lagoon a week earlier, had the submarine in tow.

Once the *Flier* was inspected and deemed seaworthy enough to be moved, the USS *Florikan* took the submarine in tow at 3:50 P.M. Although the *Flier*'s port propeller shaft was out of commission, it was believed that the starboard shaft might be used in an emergency. The *Florikan* set off from Midway at 4:52 P.M., pulling the *Flier* along at a sluggish eight knots. The submarine chaser USS *PC-602* acted as an escort, armed with depth charges, one three-inch gun, and two 20 mm guns. Since the *Flier* was incapable of diving, it offered the Japanese an easy target.

As the *Flier* was heading home to Pearl Harbor, the *Macaw* remained hard aground. When the submarine USS *Halibut* arrived at Midway on the morning of 1 February, the aftereffects of the *Flier*'s grounding remained all too evident. Owing to rough weather, the Midway Channel was closed, and the *Halibut* had to ride out the next twenty-four hours before being allowed to enter the sheltered atoll. When the *Halibut*'s commander, Ignatius J. "Pete" Galantin, finally conned his vessel up the channel, he passed the stranded hulk of the *Macaw*. Galantin and the *Macaw*'s skipper had been classmates at the Naval Academy and the Submarine School.[12]

Attempts to salvage the *Macaw* did not go well. Storms continued to rage, at times sweeping the ship with thirty-foot seas. In the early hours of 13 February, the *Macaw* began to list and slide back into deeper water. With the hull breached, the *Macaw* sank. Most of the crew managed to survive by clinging to life buoys or to the reef itself, but there were five fatalities. The dead included the *Macaw*'s skipper, Paul Burton.

The wreck of the *Macaw* stood as a grim reminder of Midway's hazards. When the USS *Tang* arrived at the atoll on 3 March 1944, skipper Richard O'Kane steered gingerly past the protruding masts of the sunken ship. In rough weather some submarines elected to bypass Midway altogether rather than risk the *Flier*'s fate. Eventually the *Macaw*'s hulk threatened to block the south channel, and salvage divers from the USS *Shackle* used demolition charges and underwater cutting to break it up. Today the twisted wreckage and the relatively intact bow still lie on the ocean floor.[13]

6

Board of Investigation

The *Flier*'s tow back to Pearl Harbor was not without incident. The day after leaving Midway, 23 January 1944, the ships encountered a severe storm in the predawn hours. At 5:42 A.M. the towline to the *Florikan* separated, leaving the *Flier* wallowing in the rough seas. The *Flier* tried to regain some steerage using the starboard screw, but it continued to drift. It took five hours under "the most adverse circumstances" to shackle up a new towline. John Crowley praised the efforts of the *Florikan*'s commander, George Sharp, as well as the work of several of his own crew, including Ensign Herbert "Teddy" Baehr, chief gunner's mate Charles De-Witt Pope, and coxswain Gale Winstone Hardy. At one point Pope was washed overboard, but he was quickly hauled back aboard by his lifeline.[1]

Despite such heroics, the *Flier*'s crew must have felt a profound ambivalence. When they reached the submarine base at Pearl Harbor on the afternoon of 30 January 1944, there was no brass band waiting dockside to greet them. This was an ignominious return from a patrol of self-destruction.

Sharp, at least, would get some recognition for his part in returning the *Flier* safely: he would be given a second chance at commanding a submarine. Sharp had been summarily relieved of command of the USS *Spearfish* after a bungled attack on a massive Japanese convoy in June 1943. Bringing the *Flier* back in one piece had wiped the slate clean, and Sharp replaced William Davis Irvin as skipper of the *Nautilus*. Soon he would be operating out of Australia on "special missions" to the Philippines.[2] Whether Crowley would be given another chance to command was still undecided, pending an investigation.

Charles Lockwood, commander of the Submarine Force Pacific Fleet, instructed Captain John Bailey Longstaff, commander of Submarine Squadron Fourteen, to convene a board of investigation to look into the *Flier*'s grounding at Midway. Also appointed to the board were Captain Frank Thomas Watkins, Captain William Vincent O'Reagan, and Lieutenant Commander Ralph B. Johnson. Watkins had distinguished himself by becoming the first division commander to skipper a submarine, taking the *Flying Fish* out on patrol in mid-1943. At the age of forty-five, he was also the oldest American to captain a submarine during the war. He was credited with sinking a ship off Formosa and received a Bronze Star for his trouble.[3]

The inquiry was held on the tender USS *Bushnell* (AS-15), which had been launched by the Mare Island Navy Yard in September 1942 and commissioned on 10 April 1943. Displacing almost 10,000 tons, the ship was more than 530 feet long with a 73-foot beam. Eventually the *Bushnell* would serve as a submarine tender at Majuro, Midway, and Guam. In the meantime, having arrived at Pearl Harbor in July 1943, the *Bushnell* tended Longstaff's squadron. With the squadron and divisional staff domiciled on the ship, the members of the board could virtually step from their bunks to the inquiry.[4]

Crowley was officially notified of the proceedings and of his "status of defendant." By naval tradition, the skipper was ultimately responsible for all decisions, and Crowley was no doubt aware that his career and reputation were at stake. Next to a court-martial, a board of investigation was the most serious proceeding an officer could face. Before the war, any skipper who grounded his ship automatically and immediately lost his command, as well as any chance of future promotion. For instance, after the grounding of the submarine USS *Razorback* at Fisher's Island off Portsmouth, both the skipper and the executive officer were relieved of command and put on disciplinary leave.[5]

The *Flier* was certainly not the first craft—or even the first submarine—to come to grief on a reef at Midway. After a refit at Midway in mid-1943, the USS *Scorpion* ran aground during training for its third war patrol. It took a tugboat five hours to pull the submarine free of the reef, and then, because of rough weather, the *Scorpion* had to wait another three days before returning to the Midway base. From there it sailed back to Pearl Harbor for repairs and an immediate board of investigation. The *Scorpion*'s skipper, William Naylor Wylie, as well as executive officer Harry Clark Maynard, were subsequently relieved of command.[6] That was not the outcome Crowley was hoping for.

The board of investigation met for the first time on Tuesday, 1 February. Crowley, who had arrived at Pearl Harbor less than forty-eight hours earlier, was present at 9:00 A.M. He waived his right to counsel and, at his request, was sworn in as a witness. After Crowley read a narrative of the events that he believed led to the *Flier*'s grounding, the board went to personally inspect the damage to the submarine at the navy yard dry dock. There was major damage to large sections of the outer hull plating; the flat keel, vertical keel, and bilge keels; the rudder, port strut, port propeller shaft, and both propellers; the main ballast tank; and the variable tank flood valves. There was moderate damage to part of the hull frames and tank bulkheads, the stern tubes and reduction gears, the liquidometer, and the Fathometer. In addition, the main engine saltwater cooling system was clogged with coral sand. The navy yard at Pearl Harbor estimated the cost of repairs at a staggering (by 1944 standards) $312,000.[7]

When the board reconvened at 1:15 in the afternoon, Crowley was questioned at length about the *Flier*'s grounding. When asked whether he had ever considered delaying the submarine's entry into Midway Channel due to the weather and sea conditions, Crowley replied, it "crossed my mind."[8] But since a pilot had been sent out and the *Flier* had been assigned a berth in the harbor, he believed that the channel was considered safe. Neither Crowley nor his navigator had been to Midway before, so he had relied on what he assumed to be more competent local knowledge.

The following morning the board interviewed the *Flier*'s executive officer, Benjamin Ernest Adams Jr. A defiant Adams told the board that he firmly believed the *Flier* had been *in* the channel when it grounded. When asked how he could reconcile this belief with the wreck, Adams suggested that the high seas combined with materials from dredging operations at Midway had created an obstruction.[9]

The board continued to interview other personnel, including officers from the navy yard who reported on the *Flier*'s damage. On Saturday, the fifth day of the inquiry, Crowley asked to be recalled to testify on his own behalf. He had clearly had time to reflect on the situation and his previous testimony, and he wanted to get his subsequent thoughts on the record. Crowley told the board that although he accepted responsibility for the decision to enter Midway Channel, he wanted to explain the factors that had influenced his decision. He noted again his lack of experience with local conditions and reiterated that if the authorities at Midway expected him to enter the harbor, he had to assume that doing so would be safe. He also assumed, once it became clear that a pilot could not be transferred to the submarine, that following the pilot boat into the lagoon was an acceptable alternative. Crowley also subscribed to the explanation offered by his executive officer: when the *Flier* struck the reef, he believed that it was in Midway Channel. This belief was fostered by the fact that one of the channel buoys was missing and another eastern buoy was out of position, presumably due to the rough conditions.[10]

The wait for the board's findings was mercifully brief. The board members deliberated on Sunday morning and again on

Monday, and on Tuesday, 8 February, they handed down their decision.

The board concluded that Crowley's decision to enter Midway Channel had been correct. In their opinion, reduced visibility due to the weather had not been an important factor, but the missing channel buoy and the sea conditions had made controlling the *Flier* "exceedingly difficult." They did, however, fault Crowley for entering the channel at the relatively low speed of ten knots. In addition, the board considered it proper for Crowley to order the anchor detail to the submarine's deck and did not find it "blame worthy" that the men in the detail had not been wearing life belts. With some ambiguity, the board of investigation concluded that Commander Crowley "is responsible for the grounding of U.S.S. *Flier*," but "the grounding was not due to the culpable negligence of any person."[11]

Vice Admiral Charles Lockwood had to sign off on the report, and he was not quite as forgiving. Lockwood was one of the icons of the U.S. submarine service, having served since World War I. As such, he had played a significant role in the evolution of both its equipment and its ethos. Among the men under his charge, he was popularly known as "Uncle Charlie," and although he could be tough when warranted, he had a reputation for fairness. For all these reasons, Lockwood's opinions were highly regarded.

In his cover letter on the board's findings, Lockwood noted that there was no evidence that the *Flier* had been "ordered" to enter Midway Channel. Even if such evidence existed, it remained Crowley's responsibility as skipper to exercise his own discretion in safeguarding his vessel. Lockwood further implied that, given the sea conditions, the anchor detail should have been wearing life preservers. Although Lockwood believed that Crowley had "committed an error in judgment," he found the decision to enter the channel "excusable." Lockwood concluded, "No further action is recommended nor contemplated."[12]

The controversy over the lack of life preservers would have an intriguing postscript. Earl Baumgart later claimed that one of his crewmates had been pressured to testify that the men who went topside had been wearing life preservers. The crewman alluded to was Donald P. Tremaine, a veteran of the Pearl Harbor attack while serving on the USS *Maryland*. Just who pressured Tremaine to give false testimony is unclear, but Baumgart claimed that Tremaine "was very bitter about the whole incident."[13]

Tremaine never appeared before the board, but the testimony of other *Flier* crewmen was somewhat ambiguous on the issue of life preservers. James Liddell, officer of the deck when the *Flier* grounded, was questioned at length about the use of life belts. He stated that he did not know whether any of the men in the anchor detail had been wearing them. Although he had given the order, at the captain's direction, to send life belts to the bridge, he could not be sure whether this had been before or after sending the anchor detail on deck. Liddell conceded that as officer of the deck it had been his responsibility to equip the men with life belts, but before the grounding, he had not believed that conditions warranted doing so.[14]

Ensign Baehr, who had been in charge of the anchor detail, testified that the men had not been wearing life belts. The board also interviewed Kenneth Gwinn, chief torpedoman's mate and part of the anchor detail. Gwinn indicated that although life belts had been available when they first tried to drop the anchor, he "did not figure we would need them." George Banchero, motor machinist's mate second class, stated that he had not seen any of the men from the anchor party taking life belts.[15]

This evidence seemed to be contradicted by the testimony of Joseph Lia, torpedoman's mate third class. He told the board that although James Cahl had been wearing a life belt, he was unsure whether it had been inflated. Waite Hoyt Daggy, fireman first class, also testified that he had been wearing a life belt and that they had been handed out when the submarine went aground. He did not know, however, whether Cahl had been wearing one. Under further questioning as to whether life belts had been made available before Cahl and Gerber went overboard, Daggy stated that although there were plenty of life belts to go around, he did not know which men took advantage of them.[16]

In summary, the evidence suggests a good deal of confusion, but it is not sufficient to indicate an attempted cover-up. There seemed to be a reluctance to wear life preservers not just on the *Flier* but throughout the navy. In the northern latitudes there was little point, since even a short time in the icy waters meant certain death. More generally, some sailors took the view that donning life belts was tantamount to admitting defeat. Or perhaps their reluctance was simply indicative of a broader fatalism, with many submariners assuming that all would survive or all would be lost. Indeed, many of them doubted that they would make it through the war alive.[17]

John Crowley thus survived the investigation and would command the *Flier* another day. His first patrol in the new submarine, however, had come at a high price. One member of his crew was dead, and five men from the USS *Macaw* lost their lives as an indirect result of the *Flier*'s grounding.

Eventually the findings and recommendations of the board of investigation would find their way to the secretary of the navy, who approved them on 1 September 1944.[18] By that time, the *Flier* and most of its crew were at the bottom of the sea.

7

Resumed Patrol

The work required to restore the *Flier* was beyond the scope of the navy yard at Pearl Harbor. After the submarine's starboard shaft and screw were repaired, the *Flier* limped to Mare Island off San Francisco, arriving on 25 February 1944. It would be more than two months before the *Flier* was ready to resume duty.[1]

Workers at the Mare Island shipyard had been recruited from all over the United States to staff continuous shifts that ran seven days a week. The population of adjacent Vallejo had increased fourfold following the attack on Pearl Harbor. Indeed, the population of California grew a staggering 50 percent during the 1940s. Wartime San Francisco became crowded not only with uniformed men but also with their wives, girlfriends, and families, who wanted to remain in close proximity to their loved ones in the military.[2]

For many submariners with rural or small-town backgrounds, San Francisco was a much more cosmopolitan and vibrant environment than they were accustomed to. New recruit George R. Wells recalled being shocked when the stage performers in a San Francisco nightclub turned out to be men in drag.[3] Calvin Moon, sent to California for training, characterized liberty in San Francisco as being "pretty great." He remembered, "We had a favorite bar and a restaurant we went to all the time. Met lots of girls, went to a lot of dances."[4] Service clubs and canteens proliferated, sponsored by such agencies as the United Service Organizations and American Women's Voluntary Services.

While in San Francisco, John Crowley kept a close eye on the *Flier*'s progress at the navy yard. More so than other ship captains, submarine commanders carefully monitored the quality of any repairs or alterations made to their vessels.[5] During the *Flier*'s repair, Crowley and executive officer Benjamin Adams had what writer Clay Blair describes as an "irreconcilable dispute."[6] Adams, originally from Wilmington, North Carolina, had gained a reputation at the Naval Academy for his sense of humor and for being a ladies' man. According to one crew member, the problem was that Adams "was not willing to work."[7] In the end, Adams was transferred to the *Albacore,* commanded by Jim Blanchard. The *Albacore* was in San Francisco for an overhaul at the time, and its executive officer, Ralph Loach, was being reassigned to a new submarine. In January 1945 Adams would be given command of the *Rasher* for its sixth patrol.

On the *Flier,* James Liddell took Adams's place as executive officer. Liddell, originally from Pennsylvania, had been an all-American football player at Northwestern University in Illinois. Also joining the *Flier*'s wardroom at Mare Island was Ensign Alvin E. Jacobson Jr. Born and raised in Grand Haven on Lake Michigan, he found San Francisco "a great party town."[8] Growing up near the water, Jacobson had become involved in sailboat racing at a young age. Later he attended the University of Michigan at Ann Arbor, completing a degree in mechanical engineering. While at the university he joined the naval reserve officer training program and was commissioned an ensign on graduation. After volunteering for submarine duty, he attended the Submarine School at New London for three months. From there he was sent to Mare Island and reported to the *Flier* on 15 April. Jacobson became the submarine's youngest officer.

After returning to Pearl Harbor on 8 May 1944, the *Flier* spent two weeks in training before resuming its first war patrol on 21 May. Not surprisingly, in later accounts Crowley rarely mentioned

The Southwest Pacific

the initial phase of the patrol and its disastrous interruption at Midway. This time the *Flier* refueled at Johnston Island, some 720 miles southwest of Pearl Harbor. The crew then set course to patrol the Philippine waters west of Luzon, terminating at Fremantle, Western Australia.

Crowley no doubt felt pressure to have a successful patrol. A cash prize of $15 and a quart of Old Taylor bourbon were offered to the first lookout that spotted an enemy target. Typically the *Flier* kept four lookouts on the bridge, both day and night. On the

surface there was a continuous high periscope watch; when submerged they generally ran at periscope depth, checking the surface
at least every ten minutes. There was also a continuous watch on
sound and radar. The *Flier*'s officers considered themselves lucky
to have a good radar operator who was usually able to detect the
size of a ship from the radar pip.[9]

The first sighting of the enemy came on 4 June, when the crew
picked up a convoy (designated 375) west of the Bonin Islands,
traveling from the Marianas to Japan. The *Flier* started to pursue
the convoy on the surface under a bright moon. Crowley dived
the boat when it looked like the convoy was changing course, but
this proved to be a mistake, and they lost contact. The *Flier* resur-
faced and tried to make an end-around maneuver for an attack.
The standard strategy for U.S. submarines was to race ahead of a
potential target on the surface and then dive for a torpedo attack
once a favorable position had been obtained. The *Flier* managed to
catch up with the convoy southwest of Iwo Jima just as day broke
at about 5:00 A.M. Finding its way between the columns of the
convoy, the *Flier* lined up two targets and then fired two spreads of
three torpedoes each. There were three hits. When last seen, one of
the ships was billowing smoke amidships, and the other appeared
to be stalled in the water.[10]

As the *Flier* swung to fire its stern tubes, the crew discovered
that a ship was bearing down and attempting to ram them. Crowley ordered the submarine deep. In the ensuing attack a total of
thirty-four depth charges, believed to originate from four different
Japanese escort ships, were directed at the *Flier*. On the surface the
exploding depth charges threw up massive columns of water. Below the surface the *Flier* went to silent running and remained in one
position. Everything was switched to hand controls as mechanical
devices were shut down, and minimal lighting was used to conserve battery power. With the air-conditioning shut off, the heat
in the submarine quickly became stifling. Alvin Jacobson recalled
that he stripped off most of his clothes and sat in the dark.[11]

Submarines were vulnerable to innumerable faults and accidents, but the direct assault of a depth charge attack was what

crews feared most. Various attempts had been made to capture the experience in words. One submariner compared the shock wave from a depth charge to tons of gravel being thrown against the hull. Another described the experience as like being in a garbage can while it was beaten with a club. It is possible that the crew of the *Flier* had experienced an "indoctrinatory" depth charge as part of their training at Pearl Harbor.[12] It is doubtful, however, that this soothed their nerves when they faced the real thing.

When the *Flier* surfaced three hours later, there were still anti-submarine vessels in the vicinity. Although the rest of the convoy had escaped, there was ample evidence of the damage inflicted by the *Flier* before it went deep. When they passed through the area the next morning, the men saw lots of debris and recovered two Japanese life buoys as souvenirs. They also retrieved some documents from a lifeboat. The successful attack was a huge shot in the arm for the crew's morale. It also lifted Crowley's status. As one German U-boat officer explained, "Every hit you scored was a kind of vindication of yourself to the crew."[13]

One of the ships torpedoed and later confirmed sunk was the 10,380-ton transport *Hakusan Maru*. Built in Japan in 1923, the ship had originally been designed as a first-class liner with a total capacity of 375 passengers and crew. The *Hakusan Maru* had plied the route between Yokohama and Hamburg before becoming a Japanese troop transport. Coincidentally, it had carried 550 troops as part of the Japanese invasion of Kiska while Crowley was commanding the *S-28* in the Aleutians.[14]

On 13 June the *Flier* encountered another Japanese convoy hugging the west coast of Luzon. The eleven ships were being protected by at least half a dozen escorts. Only half a mile from shore, the convoy was protected by the shallow waters and presented a difficult target. In addition, it was midafternoon, and any approach was made more difficult by a smooth sea and a clear, sunny sky. Despite these handicaps, the *Flier* managed to work its way inside the escorts and between the columns of ships. The submarine fired its four stern tubes at a medium-sized tanker estimated to be 10,000 tons. The crew heard two timed hits, and according to Crowley, the ship "exploded violently."[15] The fate of the tanker, the 5,135-ton *Marifu Maru,* is unclear. Although it was almost certainly damaged by the *Flier*'s attack, postwar investigations attributed its sinking to aircraft from the carrier *Ticonderoga* on 6 November 1944.[16]

Before the submarine could set up on another target, the periscope was ducked underwater owing to a misunderstood order to the diving officer. The *Flier* continued to dive, however, since the instruments were picking up the sound of Japanese escorts converging from all directions. At this critical juncture, the power on the stern planes failed, causing "a few bad moments," as the patrol report nonchalantly phrased it.[17] Fortunately, the men were able to correct the angle of the boat manually as depth charges rained down.

The depth charges continued for two hours, and the crew would eventually count at least 105 explosions. It was the most severe attack the submarine had experienced, and it may have involved more than six antisubmarine craft. Trapped in a stretch of water less than a mile wide between the convoy and the shore, the *Flier* had only limited room to maneuver. The crew constantly changed course and speed in an attempt to evade the escorts. In the relatively shallow water, external noises were eerily magnified. At one point the crew could hear the propeller noises of a ship running the entire length of the *Flier*'s hull.[18] Luckily for the *Flier,* most of the depth charges were set too shallow to do serious damage. James Liddell later described the conduct of the crew during the attack as "very good."[19] Continuing underwater at two-thirds speed, the *Flier* eventually left the escorts behind.

At sunset the *Flier* surfaced and ran along the coast in an attempt to make contact with the convoy again. The submarine reached the entrance to Subic Bay without sighting the ships and then headed out to sea. Contrary to the crew's expectations, however, the convoy had also turned seaward. Although the *Flier* tried another approach on the convoy, its efforts were frustrated by air coverage, and the Japanese ships managed to reach Manila unmolested.

The *Flier* spent the next several days off Manila, close enough to see the shoreline at Bataan and Corregidor. On 21 June the crew received orders to try to intercept a portion of the Japanese fleet spotted leaving Tawi Tawi. Before the war, the island of Tawi Tawi in the Sulu Archipelago had served as a base for the U.S. Asiatic Fleet. It later became a major base for the Imperial Japanese Navy, owing to its proximity to crude oil supplies from Tarakan on Borneo.[20]

Unknown to the *Flier* crew, they were on the periphery of one of the great naval engagements of the war. The United States was planning an attack (code-named Operation Forager) on the Mariana Islands, beginning with Saipan. In the lead-up to the operation, U.S. submarines helped cut off Japanese supplies and troops. Following the attack on Saipan on 16 June, the Japanese counteroffensive developed into the Battle of the Philippine Sea. Like the earlier Battle of Midway, this Allied victory proved to be one of the turning points of the war. The Japanese fleet lost hundreds of irreplaceable aircraft and aviators. With the capture of Saipan, the Japanese home islands came within range of both propaganda radio broadcasts and American bombers. For the first time, many Japanese began to accept the reality of their inevitable defeat.[21]

On 22 June, just before sunset, the *Flier* encountered yet another convoy heading north in Mindoro Strait. Crowley let the ships roar by while the *Flier* remained submerged. After nightfall, on what Crowley later described as "a beautifully dark, clear night," the submarine surfaced and gave chase.[22] When the *Flier* caught up with the convoy west of Mindoro, the crew estimated that it included seven to nine ships with at least six escorts. The *Flier* fired six torpedoes from the bow tubes at the first two ships in the nearest column. Crowley recorded seeing two torpedoes hit the first ship aft and a third torpedo hit the second target. As junior officer of the deck, Ensign Alvin Jacobson watched the action from the after-cigarette deck. He saw two huge geysers of water shoot up from the first ship, described as a large freighter. Another geyser erupted from a second freighter, and he heard another torpedo explosion.[23] Both ships dropped out of the convoy and headed toward land. One of the ships disappeared from the *Flier*'s radar, leading to the optimistic speculation that it sank.

Although there were many Japanese escorts, most appeared to be small patrol boats, and they failed to spot the submarine. The escorts began to drop depth charges indiscriminately, which the *Flier* easily evaded while still on the surface. The *Flier*'s crew reloaded the forward torpedo tubes and began another attack forty-five minutes later, shortly after midnight. They fired four torpedoes at a medium-sized freighter. Three explosions followed, and Crowley observed two of the torpedoes hit the target. The freighter was smoking badly and began to sink at the stern, as the other ships in the convoy sailed past it.

The *Flier* was down to its last four stern torpedoes. After again evading the Japanese escorts, the submarine made another approach. The radar indicated a crippled ship, believed to have been damaged in the first attack, dead in the water about three miles from the shore. The *Flier* headed toward the ship, intending to finish it off, but this time the escorts kept the sub at bay. Nevertheless, the sound crew later reported the distinctive noises of a ship breaking up, which they assumed was the crippled ship sinking. With three ships sunk or damaged, it had been a good night's work. James Liddell later reflected on that night of action as his "most exciting and most satisfying war experience."[24] Japanese records, however, indicated that the *Flier* had torpedoed only one ship in the attack, resulting in moderate damage to the 5,838-ton army cargo ship *Belgium Maru*.[25]

After reporting the results of its work to the task force commander, the *Flier* was ordered to proceed to Fremantle. To celebrate heading in, the men feasted on their remaining provisions of meat, fresh vegetables, and strawberry shortcake.[26] This would be a far different "homecoming" than the one following the first phase of the patrol. The *Flier* was credited with sinking four freighters, for a total of 19,500 tons. It was also credited with damaging an additional freighter and tanker, totaling 13,500 tons.[27] That was a successful patrol by anyone's standards, and Rear Admiral Ralph Christie, commander of submarines in the Southwest Pacific, wrote a glowing endorsement. Christie complimented the submarine's "excellent area coverage" and noted that "in spite of intensive counter-measures, *Flier* successfully completed four aggressive and skilful attacks." A second patrol endorsement by H. H. McLean, commander of Submarine Squadron Sixteen, also used the magic word *aggressive*.[28] This would have been music to any skipper's ears, but given the grounding at Midway and Crowley's lack of success with the *S-28*, such praise must have boosted his confidence enormously.

The combined tonnage qualified Crowley for a Navy Cross, the navy's second highest combat decoration. By this time, sinking a designated number of ships more or less guaranteed a submarine skipper the Navy Cross, although some believed that the decorations were given too liberally. In 1943 Fleet Admiral Ernest King lamented that "too many Navy Crosses have been awarded for acts which are *not* in the category of being 'next door' to the requirements for the award of the Medal of Honor."[29]

After the war the Joint Army-Navy Assessment Committee (JANAC) considerably whittled down the *Flier*'s combat record when it tallied the number of ships sunk. The submarine received credit for only one confirmed sinking—the transport *Hakusan Maru*, which went down west of the Bonins in the Philippine Sea.[30] Such discrepancies in the number of ships claimed and later confirmed by JANAC were extremely common and sometimes hotly contested. A few submarine skippers may have deliberately exaggerated the number of "kills," but in most cases it was simply that perceptions had been distorted by the heat of battle and wishful thinking. Night actions in particular resulted in phantom ships sunk. Faulty torpedoes were another common cause of misinterpreted explosions. A torpedo exploding prematurely, as they often did, could mimic a hit on an enemy ship, resulting in the same explosive column of water and heeling over of the target. Exploding depth charges could also be misinterpreted as the death throes of an enemy ship.[31]

In the *Flier*'s case, a combination of these factors may explain the difference between the number of enemy ships claimed and the number eventually confirmed by JANAC. For the time being, though, the crew had every reason to celebrate a highly successful patrol.

8

Fremantle

The *Flier* ended its patrol at Fremantle, arriving at noon on Wednesday, 5 July 1944. After spending forty-seven days on patrol and traveling 10,552 miles, the *Flier* had only 100 gallons of fuel left when it reached port.[1]

The crew, like so many before them, received a warm reception. Although it was the middle of winter in Western Australia, temperatures could still climb to the sixties and seventies during the day. Apart from the inverted seasons, visiting Americans were often struck by what one U.S. journalist described as a nation "sturdily loyal to its British traditions and ancestry."[2] Even so, the day before the *Flier* arrived, many buildings in Western Australia had flown American flags to commemorate Independence Day, and the state's premier had broadcast a formal message of thanks for U.S. assistance during the war.[3]

Although Australia had followed Britain into the war in 1939, Japan's involvement and the fall of Singapore in February 1942 had led to fears of imminent invasion. Prime Minister John Curtin told his fellow Australians that they faced "the gravest hour in our history."[4] Shirley Ingram from Swanbourne, a seaside suburb of Perth, recalled her terror after overhearing a conversation between her mother and the next-door neighbor. Her mother, who had already lost her serviceman husband in the Battle of El Alamein, confided, "If the Japs come I will kill the girls."[5]

With Australian troops concentrated overseas, many Western Australians welcomed the arrival of U.S. submarines to provide them with some desperately needed protection. Norma Black Royle was taking a bus to her job in Perth in March 1942 when she and the other passengers spotted ships on the horizon. Assuming that the ships were Japanese, the bus driver pulled over to the side of the road and announced that he was returning to the southern town of Rockingham to be with his family. As it turned out, they were not Japanese ships but U.S. submarines. Royle reported that soon the streets of Perth were crowded with American sailors—"it seemed to me as if a few hundred Clark Gables, Gene Kellys, and Robert Taylors had rolled into town."[6]

The Australians had no submarines of their own, but Fremantle and the nearby city of Perth provided excellent infrastructure for a submarine base. The port could store nearly 1 million barrels of fuel. There were also machine shops for repairs, and in September 1942 a slipway was completed for servicing Allied submarines. The American fleet boats were too large to be winched entirely out of the water, so divers were still needed to complete repairs on the underwater portions. By the time the *Flier* arrived, there were some 200 Australian civilians employed at the submarine facilities.[7] More important from the submariners' point of view, there were abundant recreational facilities and a friendly local population.

Fremantle acquired an almost mythic status among American submariners. When Bill Gleason from the USS *Gurnard* arrived in May 1943, he noted in his diary that Western Australia was "the Sub sailor's (so I hear) heaven."[8] William Godfrey, who arrived on the *Kraken*, recalled: "The best place of all was Fremantle, Australia. That was a Mecca. That was a great place. And, they received the Yanks with open arms."[9] Admiral Charles Lockwood would later claim, "The request I received most often by Pacific Fleet submarine skippers was to be allowed to end their patrol run in Fremantle."[10] Many American submariners would speak with affection of Western Australia for the rest of their lives.

Those in the Australian armed forces took a more cynical view of the Americans and their status as saviors. As early as March 1942, Brian Ogle, an Australian sailor who arrived at Fremantle on the HMAS *Maryborough,* complained that Western Australia "was inundated with American servicemen who commandeered everything in sight."[11] In fact, shortages of food and other commodities predated the Americans' arrival. Starting in 1939 ships full of Australian and New Zealand troops passed through Fremantle on their way overseas, straining local resources.[12] Compared with the American presence in eastern Australia, and especially Brisbane, there were relatively few U.S. troops in Western Australia.

For American submariners, the fact that they had Fremantle and Perth pretty much to themselves was one of the features they appreciated most about Western Australia. Despite the ambience of paradise in Hawaii, the number of military personnel there—approaching half a million by 1944—swamped the civilians. On the island of Oahu, for instance, sailors competed for bar space and schemed to avoid the plethora of shore patrols. Forest J. Sterling from the *Wahoo* typically complained about the lack of liquor and the few diversions in a place "overcrowded with thousands of servicemen."[13]

Another advantage of Australia was its female population. Unlike in Hawaii, where there seemed to be few unattached women, Perth offered an abundance of attractive English-speaking women eager for male companionship. As a naïve Perth teenager, Elizabeth "Betty" Thomson described the arrival of the Americans as "gorgeous." She liked their accents, and even more, she liked the way they smelled—a combination of aftershave and chewing gum that was apparently foreign to most Australian males at the time. She attended supervised Red Cross functions at the Swan Dive, where the attractions included Coca Cola and ice cream with chocolate sauce. Although her Scottish parents forbade her to date, she soon struck up an acquaintance with a nineteen-year-old submariner from Latimer, Iowa, named Lee Faber. Eventually Lee became virtually one of the family.[14]

Marriages between American servicemen and local women began almost immediately after the first submarines arrived. Mary Hodgkin, an English refugee from Kuala Lumpur, wrote to her parents from Perth in May 1942 that "a daughter of a neighbour married an American sailor (everyone is doing it here!)."[15] During the *Flier*'s refit in Western Australia it was reported that, on average, two U.S. sailors a day requested permission to marry their local sweethearts. Some labeled this escalating marriage rate the "war disease." A few days after the *Flier* departed for its next patrol, the American Red Cross sponsored an informational meeting for the many Australian brides and fiancées of American sailors.[16]

At the same time, the local tabloid newspaper, the *Mirror*, stirred up moral outrage about U.S. servicemen allegedly wrecking Australian marriages. According to the *Mirror*, many American sailors had been named as corespondents in divorce cases in which Australian women were accused of having adulterous affairs. The newspaper further claimed that the U.S. Navy helped run interference for those sailors as they tried to evade process servers.[17] Such stories apparently did little to dampen the enthusiasm of local women, however, and the mutual attraction persisted well after the war. When the World War II vintage submarine the *Archerfish* visited Fremantle in 1961, at least four crewmen married women they met in Australia.[18]

The first commander of submarines at Fremantle, Captain John Wilkes, remained in Western Australia only briefly. Long overdue for rotation, he was succeeded by Charles Lockwood. Following the untimely death of Admiral Robert English in an air crash in early 1943, Lockwood was precipitously promoted to vice admiral and received orders on 5 February 1943 to take command of submarines at Pearl Harbor. Ralph Waldo Christie replaced Lockwood at Fremantle, moving from Brisbane, where he had been responsible for U.S. submarines since April 1942. Like Lockwood, Christie was steeped in submarine culture dating back to World War I.

Under normal circumstances, Christie would have met the *Flier* at the Fremantle wharf when it arrived on 5 July. But as it happened, Christie was taking care of pressing business elsewhere. Admiral Christie had been waiting at the northern port of Darwin on 21 June when the USS *Harder* returned from one of the most celebrated submarine patrols of the war. The *Harder* had left Fremantle a month earlier on a special mission to extract a party of Australian commandos trapped in Borneo. In addition to rescuing the commandos, the *Harder*'s crew claimed the sinking of five Japanese destroyers along the way. Christie thought it would be useful for him to continue on a brief patrol with the submarine after it reloaded with torpedoes at Darwin. The extended patrol failed to sink any additional ships, and Christie returned to Darwin on 3 July. Two days later, the same day the *Flier* arrived at Fremantle, Christie was at a high-level conference with Lockwood in Brisbane.[19]

The Brisbane conference had been recommended by Admiral Chester Nimitz, and its main purpose was to work out some coordinating problems between the submarines under Lockwood's authority and those under Christie. The meetings did iron out some of the practical issues resulting from a divided command, but they also underlined the strained personal relationship between Lockwood and Christie. In his diary, Christie railed against what he considered Lockwood's "witless jokes and personal remarks." He would later characterize Lockwood as arrogant and egotistical and as having "a superior English-type sense of humour."[20]

Apart from their differences in personality, the main issue that divided Lockwood and Christie was the state of American torpedoes. Having completed an advanced degree at the Massachusetts Institute of Technology, Christie had been intimately involved in the U.S. torpedo program before the war. Development had been carried out mainly by the Research Department of the Naval Torpedo Station at Newport, and according to one critic, the torpedo station "had stultified in layers of bureaucratic mold."[21] Once the United States entered World War II, the defects in the torpedoes became all too apparent to many submarine skippers and their

crews. While commanding submarines in Western Australia, Lockwood had conducted his own torpedo tests and established that
they ran much deeper than set. This was only one of a number of
defects eventually discovered.

For his part, Christie remained a staunch defender of the torpedoes, attributing most of the problems to human error. Not un-
reasonably, he argued that skippers were reporting about torpedo
performance under far less than ideal conditions. More often than
not, after firing their torpedoes, commanders ordered their boats
deep to evade detection. They were hardly in a position to make
close observations of torpedo performance. Myriad things could
go wrong, apart from defects in the torpedoes themselves. Some
problems could be attributed to poor maintenance practices, and
there was always the possibility of enemy sabotage.[22]

There is indeed evidence that some of these factors influenced
torpedo performance. Skipper Charles "Herb" Andrews recalled
one occasion when he ordered the firing of four torpedoes but
later discovered that his executive officer had failed to enter the
data from the torpedo data computer or to arm the weapons. On
another occasion on the USS *Dace*, the maintenance crew left a
screwdriver in one of the torpedoes.[23] Despite such incidents, however, there is overwhelming evidence that the navy's torpedoes had
inherent faults for much of the war.

By mid-1943 the strain between Lockwood and Christie over
the torpedo issue was evident in their correspondence. Christie
was livid that Lockwood had officially endorsed skippers' claims
about defective torpedoes in his comments on their patrol reports.
He wrote to Lockwood: "What conceivable good such a remark
can do is beyond me but it is not beyond me to appreciate the very
definite harm that can be done and has been done."[24] Lockwood's
reply took a mocking tone: "From the amount of belly-aching it
[Christie's letter] contains, I assume that the breakfast coffee was
scorched or perhaps it was a bad egg."[25] Christie subsequently
backed off, and Lockwood conceded that perhaps he had been "a
little touchy," although he still referred to Christie's letter as "very
snotty." In the same letter, Lockwood concluded: "We are all on

the same team and I for one intend to keep personalities out of the problem to the maximum degree."[26]

By the time of the *Flier*'s patrol, most of the torpedo problems had been resolved. Even so, continuing defects may help explain the discrepancies between the ships Crowley thought he sank and the number that could be confirmed later. Nevertheless, Crowley and his crew had good reason to celebrate their accomplishments when they arrived at Fremantle. Among the movies being screened in Perth during the *Flier*'s stay was the new James Cagney feature *Johnny Come Lately*. Given the debacle at Midway and the subsequent success in the Philippine Sea, Crowley may well have identified with the title and with the sentiment of the advertising, which proclaimed, "Cagney's back in action."[27]

With two weeks of recreational leave ahead of them, the men had plenty of opportunities to go to the movies, attend dances, and enjoy other pursuits. A number of submariners escaped the city and headed for more provincial towns such as Kalgoorlie and Albany. Some crewmen borrowed firearms from the *Flier* to go rabbit shooting or on kangaroo hunts.[28] After months of enforced sobriety at sea, many submariners looked forward to imbibing large amounts of alcohol. Submarine officers were issued a couple of bottles of spirits and a case of beer. William Godfrey from the *Kraken* received forty-eight quart bottles of Emu Bitter ("the finest beer I ever drank," he remembers fondly) in a wooden crate. He and the other *Kraken* officers pooled their beer and had all they could drink for the next two weeks.[29]

Alvin Jacobson, acting as officer of the bridge, had to bail some of the crew out of trouble during their leave. One of the *Flier*'s chiefs was arrested for urinating in the middle of a street, and Jacobson had to get him out of jail.[30] Earl Baumgart became another casualty of the leave in Australia when his conduct resulted in a reduction in rank from motor machinist's mate to fireman. He later explained, "I guess I drank too much of their strong beer." Convinced that his punishment far outweighed his offense, Baumgart was determined to ask for a transfer and fight the charges against him when they returned to base from the next patrol.[31] These concerns, however, would soon be overshadowed by the dramatic events that followed.

9

Death in Thirty Seconds

By 23 July the *Flier* crew was back on board, carrying out exercises with the *Muskallunge* and the *Gunnel* off Fremantle. What would be designated the *Flier*'s second war patrol began when the submarine departed Fremantle at 3:00 on the afternoon of Wednesday, 2 August 1944. Initially the *Flier* traveled in the company of its former training partner, the *Muskallunge,* skippered by Michael Russillo. The submarines sailed together up Australia's west coast and reached Exmouth Gulf two days later. In what had become routine for Fremantle-based submarines, they topped up their tanks from a fuel barge there.

For a time it was envisioned that Exmouth Gulf might serve as an advance submarine base, being several days closer to the war zone than Fremantle was. Both the U.S. Navy and the Royal Australian Navy established small communications stations there. Some submariners, however, considered a base at that remote spot "a screwy idea."[1] In any case, things did not go as planned. When the tender *Pelias* was stationed there in mid-1943, rough seas prevented submarines from docking alongside. To make matters worse, the Japanese began carrying out air raids on the gulf. The idea for a base was thus abandoned, but a fuel barge at Exmouth Gulf continued to be maintained for submarines on their way to patrols.[2]

The *Flier* spent the night at Exmouth Gulf, departing early the next morning. On the way out of the gulf the crew got in some target practice, firing the deck guns at an old ship that had run aground years earlier. One of the *Flier* crew claimed that the hulk had been shot at by more submarines than had any other ship in the world.[3]

Once the *Flier* passed through the Malay Barrier some 2,000 miles north of Fremantle, the submarine's instructions were to look for enemy shipping off Indochina in the South China Sea. Crowley later described the initial phase of the patrol as "uneventful."[4] But that was before the *Flier* began traversing Balabac Strait, a stretch of water linking the Sulu Sea and the South China Sea.

As the *Flier* prepared to enter Balabac Strait from the Sulu Sea, the crew received a top-secret communication known as an "ultra." Much of the information about enemy ship movements came from code breakers who intercepted Japanese communications. This information was so sensitive that only a submarine's skipper was privy to it, and he had to sign an oath that bound him to decades of secrecy.[5] By 1943 the submarine command was sending out an average of two or three ultras a day. Submarines were sometimes sent on wild-goose chases, and the odds of actually putting a torpedo in the designated target were about one in nine. Even so, it is estimated that ultras helped locate about half the Japanese merchant ships sunk.[6]

The message received by the *Flier* indicated a southbound convoy in the South China Sea. In an attempt to intercept the convoy, the *Flier* cranked up to fifteen knots, transiting Balabac Strait on the surface. Crowley stationed himself on the bridge, along with an increased number of lookouts.

At 3:00 P.M., 13 August, the *Flier* passed the heavily wooded island of Bancoran, some nineteen miles to the northeast, and entered the recommended route to Nasubata Channel. After sunset the sky became totally overcast, and the crew was unable to get a fix on any stars; instead, bearings were taken on the peaks of Balabac Island and Palawan Island to determine the *Flier*'s position. At 6:00 P.M. the submarine appeared to be on course about fifty miles from Balabac Island. The crew began taking depth soundings, and these coincided with their chart. At 9:00 P.M. they made radar contact with Comiran Island, some 16,000 yards away, and then sighted the island half an hour later. The *Flier* throttled back to five knots to confirm its position relative to the surrounding islands of Balabac, Comiran, and Roughton.

With its position apparently confirmed, the *Flier* picked up speed to seventeen knots. Crowley ordered Lieutenant William Reynolds and Ensign Phil Mayer to the bridge as extra lookouts. There were now nine men topside, including the skipper.[7] In normal circumstances there would be three lookouts (in addition to the skipper, officer of the deck, and junior officer of the deck). The navigator might also come topside from time to time to take sightings of their position.[8]

At 10:00 P.M., with Comiran Island believed to be approximately 6,700 yards away, things fell apart. As Crowley later described the events, he heard a "terrific explosion" that seemed to come from the *Flier*'s starboard side near the forward battery compartment. The force of the blast "dazed" Crowley, and when he "came to," he was clinging to the target bearing transmitter rail on the after part of the bridge. Crowley's first impulse was to move forward to sound the collision alarm, located above the conning tower hatch, but he never reached the alarm. Water swept over the bridge, and the submarine sank with "astounding rapidity." Crowley estimated that within twenty to thirty seconds the submarine was totally submerged. When Crowley later relived the horror of those moments, various sensations colored his memory. There was the overpowering smell of fuel oil and the fierce sound of air venting through the conning tower hatch. Worst of all were the screams of men from below as the vessel flooded.[9]

James Liddell, the executive officer, was in the conning tower when he heard a "muffled" explosion. He had just moved under the conning tower hatch so that he could talk to Crowley on the bridge. An eruption of air hurled him from the conning tower to the bridge with enough force to rip his shirt off. The sudden burst of air had presumably been caused by the massive ingress of seawater through the submarine's breached hull. As Liddell tried to move aft to the cigarette deck, he was in water up to his waist; then, before he knew it, he was swimming for his life. In hindsight, he was surprised that he had not been dragged under as the submarine sank.[10]

Earl Baumgart was sucked underwater as the submarine sank. He had been standing lookout above the *Flier*'s A-frame, with about twenty minutes of his watch left, when disaster struck. Suddenly he was in the water being pulled down into the vortex of the sinking submarine.[11]

Ensign Alvin E. Jacobson was also pulled fifteen or twenty feet underwater by the sinking craft. He struggled to the surface, imagining that the submarine's screws were coming straight at him. Only an hour earlier he had replaced Ensign Teddy Baehr as junior officer of the deck. From his station on the after-cigarette deck, Jacobson had been admiring the silhouette of the surrounding mountains when he got the first inkling of disaster. A tremendous gush of air burst through the conning tower hatch, and Lieutenant William Reynolds was blown back into him; Reynolds complained of a pain in his side. Jacobson's initial impression was that an air bank had let loose, but then the boat started to sink. He remembered seeing Ensign Phil Mayer dive over the side. Mayer had been in the conning tower manning the torpedo data computer, and Charles Pope was at the sonar. They both pulled themselves up by the periscope to escape. The air thrusting up from beneath the control room pushed them free of the submarine, and the next thing they knew, they were in the water. Others trying to exit the submarine apparently got caught up on the guardrail of the signal bridge.[12]

Miraculously, fourteen men made it into the water, mainly those who had been topside at the time of the explosion. This was consistent with similar submarine disasters caused by collisions or open hatches and valves. At the time, the most recent documented case was the sinking of the USS *R-12*, which went down on 12 June 1943. The vintage submarine, originally commissioned in 1919, was being used mainly for training purposes. While operating on the surface off Key West in the Florida Keys, the forward battery compartment began to flood. The submarine sank in less than a minute, taking most of the forty-eight-man crew with it, 600 feet to the bottom. There were only six survivors, and they had all been on the bridge, including the skipper, Edward L. Shelby.[13]

Although captains going down with their ships is part of naval tradition, in the case of the sinking of a surfaced submarine, the skipper was likely to survive, simply because he would probably be directing operations from the bridge. When the British submarine *Umpire* went down on 19 July 1941 after being rammed at night by a trawler, the commander was among the few survivors. Similarly, after the *S-26* collided in the dark with an escort in January 1942, the commander, Earl C. Hawk, was one of only three survivors. Later in the war the skipper of USS *Tang*, Richard O'Kane, was among the small number of survivors after his submarine was sunk by a torpedo.[14]

The last moments of the seventy-two men who rode the *Flier* to the bottom are unknown. It may be that most, if not all, drowned immediately after the submarine began flooding. Although Crowley's initial account is ambiguous on this point, it seems unlikely that he managed to sound the collision alarm. The steady "bong, bong" of the alarm signaled the closing of all watertight doors between the submarine's compartments. In December 1944 he told journalists that after the explosion he recalled "thinking that I should rush forward and sound the collision alarm. But water was pouring up my ankles and I knew there wasn't time."[15] Of course, even without the alarm, the men were trained to react instinctively and seal their compartments in the event of such an emergency. Depending on the angle of the boat, though, the solid steel doors could be difficult to pull shut.[16]

Back in 1925 the *S-51* was accidentally rammed by the coastal steamer *City of Rome* while running on the surface of Long Island Sound. The collision tore a huge hole in the submarine at the level of the battery room, and the *S-51* sank in less than sixty seconds. Only three men, all on the bridge at the time of the collision, were eventually rescued. Charles "Swede" Momsen, skipper of the *S-1*, arrived on the scene to assist, but it proved to be a futile effort. Momsen consoled himself that those on *S-51* had died quickly, but regrettably, Momsen would be proved wrong after the *S-51* was salvaged and taken to the New York Navy Yard dry dock the following year. When the bodies were exhumed, it became apparent that some of the men had died under horrific circumstances, trying to claw their way through the submarine's steel hull.[17]

The helplessness of men trapped in a sunken submarine was underlined a few years later with the loss of the *S-4*. In 1928 the submarine collided with a Coast Guard ship near Provincetown and sank in 100 feet of water. Divers could hear the tapping of survivors on the inside of the hull, but they were unable to raise the submarine or pump in fresh air. The entire crew was lost.[18]

Incidents such as these inspired Momsen's efforts to develop submarine rescue techniques. As noted earlier, the Momsen lung was used for training at the Submarine School at New London. Much later, in 1959, it would be proved that men could make a "buoyant ascent" of more than 300 feet without the use of a breathing apparatus, but at the time, Momsen's contraption was considered a submariner's best chance of making it to the surface. Momsen and Allan McCann also developed the McCann rescue chamber for men trapped below the surface. In a much publicized rescue in May 1939, Momsen personally supervised the retrieval of thirty-three survivors from the USS *Squalus* after it sank in 240 feet of water off Portsmouth, New Hampshire.[19]

Momsen continued to be an active force in the submarine service during World War II. At the time of the Japanese attack he was serving as an operations officer at Pearl Harbor. He worked on improving American torpedoes under Charles Lockwood and was awarded a Legion of Merit for his efforts. As commander of Submarine Squadron Two, he led the first American submarine wolf pack in late 1943. The wolf pack, a coordinated attack group, sank three enemy ships and garnered Momsen a Navy Cross.[20]

Although men were trained to use the Momsen lung at Submarine School, many did not take it seriously. William Godfrey Jr. thought that the idea of escaping a sunken submarine was "for the birds."[21] Decorated skipper Slade Cutter stated that training with the Momsen lung may have provided "a little sense of security," but "out there in the Pacific with the bottom at 2,000 fathoms, you don't worry much about Momsen lungs."[22]

A fatalistic attitude often prevailed in the submarine service: if a submarine went down, the chance of survival was remote. Many men apparently shared the attitude of British admiral Max Horton: "There is no margin for mistakes in submarines. You are either alive or dead."[23] To an extent, this could become a self-fulfilling prophecy. On the USS *Razorback,* for example, the submarine's escape trunk, designed to allow four men at a time to exit the submarine using Momsen lungs, was used to store potatoes.[24]

When the USS *Tang* sank by the stern in 180 feet of water on 25 October 1944, it became apparent that many of the trapped survivors had no idea how to use a Momsen lung. In the push to provide crews for the burgeoning submarine force, standards at the Submarine School had slipped. Some of the sailors on the *Tang* had made training escapes from a depth of only 10 feet; they also wasted valuable time debating how to operate the escape trunk. Despite these handicaps, five crewmen proved that escape from a sunken submarine was possible. They joined the four survivors who had been topside when the *Tang* sank, and they were all picked up by the Japanese and remained prisoners until the end of the war.[25]

It is doubtful that any of those on the *Flier* had the opportunity to use the lifesaving measures that Momsen dedicated so much of his career to developing. If Crowley was correct about the depth of the water where the *Flier* sank, those on board would have died before it hit the bottom. Any of the submarine's compartments that were sealed would have imploded under the tremendous pressure of the sea.

Assuming that the *Flier* sank in shallower water, survival for any significant time was still unlikely. The speed with which the *Flier* sank suggests that the flooding was widespread and catastrophic. If any of the *Flier* crew did manage to close the watertight doors of their compartments, however, they faced slow atmospheric poisoning. Flooding in the submarine compressed the already restricted air supply, and with each man exhaling the equivalent of a cubic foot of carbon dioxide every hour, it would not take long before the proportion of carbon dioxide in the atmosphere exceeded the critical level of 3 percent.[26] As the concentration of carbon dioxide increased, the men would experience symptoms of blurred vision, dizziness, headaches, and spasms. Their ability to concentrate and reason would quickly be compromised.

The presence of chlorine gas from the submarine's batteries further minimized the chances of survival. If Crowley was correct that the initial explosion occurred near the forward battery compartment, chlorine gas may have been released immediately. The gas, with a bleach-like odor, affected respiration and, in heavy concentrations, caused tissue damage and suffocation.[27] So although it is unknown whether there was anyone left alive on the *Flier* to attempt an escape, the odds were heavily stacked against him.

10

Cause and Effect

Why did the *Flier* sink with such destructive force? The extent to which John Crowley pondered this question in the desperate hours and days that followed is unknown, but by the time he filed his "survival report," he stated: "It is my opinion that a mine was in contact with the hull just below the waterline at the time of the explosion."[1] There were, of course, other possibilities. It is intriguing that neither Earl Baumgart nor Alvin Jacobson specifically mentioned an explosion in their firsthand narratives. Jacobson referred only to "a terrific gush of air" coming through the conning tower.[2] Baumgart stated vaguely, "I guess we hit a mine in that strait."[3]

Given the *Flier*'s mishap at Midway, it is tempting to speculate that the submarine may have hit a reef or other submerged hazard. The waters in the vicinity of Balabac Strait and Palawan Island were notorious for their shoals and coral heads, and the often deficient navigational charts supplied to American submarines magnified the hazards.[4] In addition, visibility was poor the night the *Flier* went down. Taken together, these factors make running aground a feasible explanation, and during the course of the war, four U.S. submarines ended their careers that way.

One of the most spectacular submarine groundings occurred later in the year, on 24 October 1944, when the USS *Darter* ran on to a half-mile-wide reef known as Bombay Shoal. The *Darter* was pursuing a Japanese convoy through the treacherous waters west

73

of Palawan Island, appropriately called Dangerous Ground. Besides being hazardous to traverse, much of the area was not properly charted, so the Japanese frequently sent convoys through the Palawan passage in the belief that no American submarine would venture there. That assumption proved costly. On 23 October the *Darter* sank Admiral Kurita's flagship, the heavy cruiser *Atago,* and damaged another heavy cruiser; its sister submarine the *Dace* sank a third. Those losses proved to be an ill omen for the Japanese in the lead-up to the titanic battle for Leyte Gulf following the U.S. invasion of the Philippines.

The next day the *Darter* suffered a mishap of it own. Running in overcast weather that prevented obtaining a navigational fix from the stars, the *Darter* slammed into a reef at full speed. Initially the crew thought they had been torpedoed. The force of the collision reared the *Darter*'s bow out of the water and left the entire submarine stranded like a beached whale. In the aftermath, Admiral Ralph Christie did not consider the *Darter*'s skipper, David Hayward McClintock, at fault. Christie believed that McClintock's gamble had been justified: he took a chance on pursuing a wounded Japanese ship in dangerous waters, and he lost.[5]

Crowley was apparently aware that grounding might be raised as a possible explanation for the *Flier*'s loss. He noted in his survival report that at the fatal moment there had been no tendency for the craft to lift, and its back was not broken.[6] In any case, there was no precedent for a submarine holed by coral or some other navigational hazard to sink so quickly. Another possible explanation was that the *Flier* had been hit by an enemy torpedo or, for that matter, a torpedo from a "friendly" sub. The records, however, show no evidence of any attacks by enemy or Allied vessels in the area.

Yet another possibility was that the explosion came from inside the submarine. The very batteries that allowed a submarine to propel itself underwater also posed a significant risk. Every fleet submarine had a forward and an after battery compartment, each carrying 126 lead acid cells for storing electricity. Each battery was six feet high and weighed more than 1,000 pounds. The batteries'

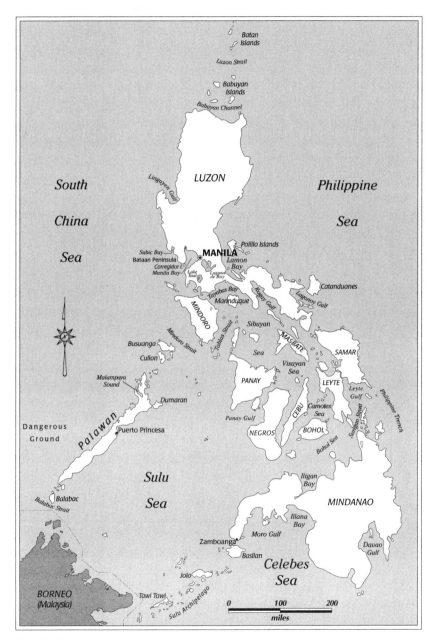

The Philippines

endurance was critical to the submarine's survival, since the ship could maneuver underwater only as long as the batteries provided power. Typically the batteries would be recharged at night while the submarine was on the surface. One of the by-products of this process was highly flammable hydrogen gas. The lower the batteries' power, the longer it took to recharge them and the greater the production of hydrogen. Even with scrupulous ventilation, pockets of hydrogen sometimes accumulated, and battery overheating or a spark could trigger a powerful explosion.[7]

Shortly after the war began, the *S-38* experienced a battery compartment explosion that injured three crewmen; one later died. Battery explosions had been implicated in other submarine disasters but had never been documented as the cause of a submarine's sinking.[8] In the postwar era, the USS *Cochino* (SS-345) was lost due to a battery explosion and fire. As the last submarine commissioned during the war, the *Cochino*'s batteries had a greater capacity compared with other World War II boats. On 25 August 1949 the submarine shuddered from an initial muffled explosion. Then, as the batteries burned, more explosions followed, and flooding began. The submarine sank in 950 feet of water off the coast of Norway.[9]

The most catastrophic submarine disaster associated with the batteries took place when the Soviet *B-37* blew up at its pier in 1961. A massive explosion erupted after the crew brought the electrical systems online, apparently igniting an accumulation of hydrogen. The blast killed fifty-nine crew members and another seventy-three people on adjacent submarines and on shore. Most of the damage, though, was done when the torpedoes detonated as a result of the fire.[10]

Alvin Jacobson recalled that in the immediate aftermath of the *Flier* disaster, the crew believed that the submarine had been sunk by a battery explosion. This was partly due to the assumed location of the damage to the submarine's hull. However, the experience of the similarly designed *Cochino* suggests that a battery explosion alone would not have sunk the *Flier* so quickly. Despite multiple explosions, the *Cochino* stayed afloat for fifteen hours.

That incident claimed the lives of six men, and the remaining crew were lost during rescue operations in horrific sea conditions.[11]

In the end, the theory that the *Flier* hit a mine remains the most compelling explanation for its loss. According to Jacobson, the *Flier* crew initially tended to dismiss this idea because they knew that other U.S. submarines had recently passed through the area. Also, the *Flier*'s sonar did not indicate the presence of any mines.[12] However, the use of frequency modulation sonar to detect mines was still in the developmental stage in mid-1944. Based on work done at the University of California War Research Laboratory in San Diego, Charles Lockwood informed Christie in late July that during recent trials, submarines had been able to pick up dummy mines at 450 yards.[13] But the equipment was not regularly installed in submarines until 1945.

Japanese records confirm the presence of mines in Balabac Strait. Soon after the attack on Pearl Harbor, the Japanese submarines *I-123* and *I-124*, two of Japan's four *Kirai Sen*–type vessels used for mine laying, were deployed in the vicinity of the Philippines. Their task included placing forty mines in Balabac Strait on 8 December 1941; they would later drop mines off Darwin, Australia, as well. The Japanese mines, known as type 88, carried 400 pounds of explosive and could arm in depths of more than 1,000 feet.

The *I-124* was sunk off Darwin on 20 January 1942 in a combined attack by the Australian minesweeper *Deloraine* and the U.S. destroyer *Edsall*. Given that the submarine sank in only forty feet of water, American divers were able to recover Japanese codebooks from the wreck—a significant breakthrough for Allied cryptanalysts. Seven months later, on 29 August, the *I-123* was spotted by an Allied aircraft in the vicinity of Guadalcanal and attacked by the destroyer-minelayer USS *Gamble*. Following a depth charge attack, the submarine sank with all hands.[14] But the *I-123* and *I-124* had already planted the seeds of their revenge.

Whether the *Flier* was brought down by a mine laid early in the war or one placed later is unclear. According to Eugene McGee, it is more likely that the *Flier* struck one of the 600 deep-sea contact mines laid in March 1944. The Japanese minelayer

Tsugaru, attached to the Third Southern Expeditionary Force, departed Palau on 24 March to carry out operations in the Balabac Strait area. It was laying type 93, model 1 mines, which could be placed in water up to 3,500 feet deep and could be set to explode at depths up to 230 feet. Each mine was housed in a floating case and anchored below the surface by a cable attached to the seabed. This type of mine presented a menace that the U.S. Navy was apparently unaware of at the time. The navy believed that moored mines were ineffective in water more than 600 feet deep. Coincidentally, the *Tsugaru* also found a watery grave. The same USS *Darter* that later grounded on Bombay Shoal torpedoed the *Tsugaru* on 29 June 1944 in the Molucca Sea, about 720 miles from Balabac Strait.[15]

As a mode of naval warfare, the use of mines can be traced back to the American Revolution, when they were essentially kegs stuffed with explosives. David Bushnell not only created the first fully functional submarine but also carried out early experiments with naval mines. On 13 August 1777, exactly 167 years before the sinking of the *Flier,* one of Bushnell's mines was launched against the British frigate *Cerberus,* sinking a nearby schooner instead of the intended target.[16]

By the time of the American Civil War, mines were being used on a fairly large scale. Barrels floating just below the surface could be fitted with contact fuses or wired to be detonated by an electrical current from shore. Sometimes they were simply towed behind ships. World War I saw the first experiments involving the deployment of mines from submarines, and German U-boats planted minefields around the British Isles with considerable success. By World War II mines had become more sophisticated. Some used electronic detectors that could respond to magnetic, pressure, or acoustic changes when ships came within range.

It is estimated that more than half a million mines were laid by submarines of all nationalities during the war. On the American side, the huge *Argonaut* was the only submarine specifically built for mine laying. The *Argonaut* could accommodate up to sixty Mark 11 mines, laying them through two tubes in the stern. Other U.S. submarines were regularly employed for mine laying or, more accurately, mine firing. Fleet submarines could eject mines from their torpedo tubes in the same way they fired torpedoes. The standard U.S. mine, the Mark 12, was twenty-one inches in diameter (the same as a torpedo) and eight feet long. A submarine could carry up to forty of these mines. Each one contained 1,200 pounds of TNT and had a delay mechanism that prevented it from arming too near the submarine that deployed it. Even so, there was always the danger of a mine going off prematurely. Each mine also had a heavy anchor at one end, which made loading them into torpedo tubes backbreaking work. These factors, along with a general feeling that submarines were best used in direct attacks on Japanese shipping, made mine laying unpopular among American crews. Lockwood professed, "Mining is something which I want to do only when the supply of torpedoes is running low."[17]

As a weapon of war, one of the advantages of mines was their relatively low cost; they were sometimes referred to as the "poor man's navy." Their effectiveness, however, was questionable. It is estimated that the Japanese deployed more than 50,000 mines in the western Pacific, but some of their best "hits" were their own ships. According to one claim, submarines of the U.S. Seventh Fleet deployed about 600 mines that sank or damaged more than fifty ships. According to W. J. Holmes, however, fewer than thirty of those ships were Japanese. In any case, mines offered other tactical advantages. They deterred enemy ships from entering certain waters, delayed shipping by compelling vessels to use alternative routes, and caused the diversion of ships and manpower for minesweeping operations. In fact, the Imperial Japanese Navy employed some 350 craft and 25,000 men for minesweeping in 1945. The mining of coastal waters could also force ships into deeper water, where they were more vulnerable to attack by submarines.[18]

The question of how many U.S. submarines became the victims of Japanese mines is also open to much conjecture. Active measures known as *deperming* and *degaussing* were taken to make submarines less susceptible to magnetic mines and torpedoes. Deperming reduced the magnetism that ships acquired during construction; it was first employed in November 1940 on the submarine *Sailfish.* In addition, submarines regularly went through the process of degaussing to neutralize their magnetic signature.[19] These measures may have been effective, but there were other types of mines that did not require a magnetic field to detonate.

Beginning in 1944 the Japanese increasingly relied on mines as an antisubmarine measure. It was not uncommon for American submarines on patrol to come across mines floating on the surface, torn from their moorings by storms. Although the Geneva conventions stipulated that unmoored mines were supposed to automatically disarm themselves, experience proved that this often was not the case. Submarine crews usually tried to explode these floating mines by shooting at them with the deck guns or small arms. During two patrols of the USS *Atule,* for example, the crew spotted fifty-two mines and managed to destroy forty-four. This could be dangerous work. The crew of the USS *Dace* was unable to detonate most of the mines they encountered, but when they did succeed in exploding one using the 20 mm gun, the shrapnel reached the deck. Floating mines remained a hazard well after the war and were blamed for damaging or sinking hundreds of ships. In fact, initial speculation was that the Russian submarine *Kursk* had hit a World War II mine, causing it to sink in August 2000.[20]

In addition to the *Flier,* it is commonly believed that as many as ten other American submarines were sunk by mines during World War II: USS *Runner,* USS *Pompano,* USS *Capelin,* USS *Scorpion,* USS *Robalo,* USS *Escolar,* USS *Albacore,* USS *Swordfish,* USS *Kete,* and USS *Bonefish.*[21] Of these, the evidence for the sinking of the *Albacore* is most conclusive. A Japanese patrol boat witnessed the submarine's death throes on 7 November 1944 after the *Albacore* struck a mine while running submerged near Esan Misaki, off the south coast of Hokkaido. Such eyewitness accounts were a rarity, however. The presumed loss of the *Scorpion* to a mine in February 1944 was based mainly on captured Japanese records documenting the presence of extensive minefields where the submarine went missing. Interestingly, the *Scorpion*'s postwar nuclear namesake would also disappear under mysterious circumstances in 1968.[22]

Along with the dearth of survivors and other witnesses, one of the things that makes the cause of a submarine's loss so difficult to pin down is the sheer number of things that might go wrong. Even without the threat of enemy action, the potential for human error and equipment failure was enormous. For instance, on 11 September 1944 the USS *Crevalle* was nearly lost when it surfaced at high speed with its main vents open. This was a fairly common practice that allowed the submarine to dive again quickly if enemy aircraft were spotted. In this case, though, the *Crevalle*'s stern planes were jammed in the dive position. Seawater swamped through the upper hatch, and the submarine headed toward the bottom. Only the self-sacrifice of the officer on the bridge, Lieutenant Howard James Blind, who managed to close the conning tower hatch, prevented that dive from being the *Crevalle*'s last.[23]

Later that same month, the USS *Narwhal* found itself in a similar predicament. While evading an enemy plane, the *Narwhal* hurtled into a runaway dive when the stern planes seized up. The submarine's downward momentum was finally stopped at 300 feet after blowing all the main ballast and backing the engines at emergency speed. Such out-of-control dives—so-called Nantucket sleigh rides—occurred with alarming regularity.[24] Many submariners had similar near-death experiences.

Of the presumed victims of enemy mines, the fate of the USS *Robalo* is especially pertinent to the loss of the *Flier*. Although the details were unknown at the time, the *Robalo* was lost two miles off the west coast of Palawan Island near Balabac Strait on 26 July 1944, only a few weeks before the sinking of the *Flier*. Earlier, while on its second war patrol, the *Robalo* had already suffered an experience similar to that of the *Crevalle* and the *Narwhal*. In that incident, a Japanese plane dropped a bomb off the *Robalo*'s port side as it dived for cover. The submarine's main induction began flooding, and the *Robalo* plunged out of control to 350 feet before regaining equilibrium.[25]

The *Robalo* departed Fremantle for its third war patrol on 22 June 1944. While traveling from Pearl Harbor to Fremantle, the *Flier* apparently crossed paths with the *Robalo* on 30 June. At about 3:00 A.M. the *Flier*'s radar picked up a craft at 7,500 yards, and the crew went to battle stations. On closer inspection the radar operator became convinced that the vessel was an American submarine, and later information led to the conclusion that it had been the USS *Robalo*.[26]

The last message from the *Robalo* was received on 2 July, when it reported sighting a Japanese battleship with escorts. Eventually it would be learned that the *Robalo* sank on 26 July, with the loss of seventy-four men. Four of the crew managed to swim two miles to the west coast of Palawan Island. They made their way through the jungle only to be captured by Japanese military police and taken to the infamous Puerto Princesa prison camp. On 2 August the *Robalo* survivors threw a note from their cell to a prison work detail. The note, which included their names and the *Robalo*'s designation number (SS-273), eventually ended up in the hands of guerrillas. On 15 August the four men from the *Robalo* were put on a Japanese patrol boat or destroyer, after which their fate is uncertain.[27] The *Robalo* crewmen believed that their submarine had gone down as a result of a battery explosion. Most commentators, however, believe that it is more likely that the *Robalo* struck a mine. The fates of both the *Robalo* and the *Flier* support this theory.

Contrary to most other submarine disasters, there was only one officer among the *Robalo*'s survivors, Ensign Samuel L. Tucker. The skipper, Manning M. Kimmel, had been given command of the *Robalo* on 29 March 1944. He was the eldest son of Admiral Husband E. Kimmel, who, as commander in chief of the Pacific Fleet in 1941, had received much of the blame for the devastation at Pearl Harbor. At President Franklin Roosevelt's direction, Admiral Kimmel had been relieved of all naval duties on 17 December 1941 and replaced by Admiral Chester Nimitz. Some, including

Ralph Christie, thought that his father's notoriety prompted Manning Kimmel to be overly aggressive in his submarine patrols. After confirmation of the *Robalo*'s loss, Christie wrote to Vice Admiral Thomas C. Kinkaid and noted in a postscript: "We had the impression that Manning was a little extra aggressive because of his Dad's P.H. experience. In fact, I warned him not to 'press.'"[28] In the end, though, it was probably not Kimmel's aggression or recklessness that sank the *Robalo* but simply bad luck.

11

Black Water

Immediately after the *Flier* sank, the survivors began to gather in the water. In the dark they shouted out their names, and fourteen men were accounted for. The ocean was mercifully warm, with a relatively low swell of about two feet. There was an oil slick, however, that discouraged them from opening their eyes or mouths. The oil clung noxiously to exposed body parts, but later this may have offered some protection from the tropical sun.[1] Alvin Jacobson, recalling his lifesaving training, stripped down to his underwear (though he later considered this a mistake). He decided to keep the binoculars that hung around his neck, since they practically floated on their own.[2]

According to executive officer James Liddell, who was interviewed in October 1944, he and John Crowley discussed a plan of action and decided to head for the nearest island. However, Crowley's various accounts differ from both Liddell's version and each other in some respects. According to Crowley's survival report, although Comiran Island was the nearest land, at an estimated three and a half miles away, they believed that Japanese soldiers were garrisoned there. Rather than risk capture, they decided to head for coral islands to the northwest. In contrast, in an account published in 1981, Crowley indicated that without stars or moonlight to guide them, it was futile to set off for land, and they agreed to tread water until the anticipated moonrise.[3]

Whatever the case, the survivors made little headway in the almost pitch-black conditions. Crowley later told a news conference, "You couldn't see three feet in front of you."[4] Occasionally a flash of lightning and a break in the clouds afforded a glimpse of land, but Crowley and Liddell agreed that they probably spent much of the night swimming in circles. Liddell noted, "I think we swam back and forth through that oil slick several times before moonrise."[5] The relatively warm water at least reduced the risk of hypothermia. Studies of rescues during the war indicated that in temperatures below forty degrees Fahrenheit, survival time in the water could be only a matter of minutes. Even at temperatures of sixty degrees, men were unlikely to survive more than five hours.[6]

By the time the moon afforded some light at approximately 3:00 A.M., a number of men had already disappeared into the black water. An early casualty was Edgar Walker Hudson, chief motor machinist's mate from Dickson, Tennessee. Among those who eventually reached land was Arthur Gibson Howell, originally from East Moriches, New York. Howell was the *Flier*'s chief radio technician, and Crowley had singled him out on the previous patrol for his excellent work with the radar system. As Howell later described the events, he tried to assist Ensign Philip Stanley Mayer, but Mayer lost consciousness after about twenty minutes in the water. Howell had to let him go, and he believed that Mayer sank below the surface.[7]

Not long after Mayer lost consciousness, Lieutenant Paul Knapp, the *Flier*'s third officer and engineer, became separated from the group. A 1942 graduate of the Naval Academy, Knapp had impressed Crowley on the first patrol by his calmness under pressure. Liddell described him as "one of the finest naval officers I have ever been associated with."[8] Knapp was also popular with the crew; Earl Baumgart characterized him as "a likeable guy, and a person you could easily communicate with."[9] Knapp had been on the bridge at the time of the explosion. Although he was initially spotted in the water, he would not be seen or heard from again.

Despite their experience at Midway, none of the men in the water wore life preservers. As noted earlier, submariners did not wear

U.S. SUBMARINE FLIER
DOWN THE WAYS
JULY 11, 1943
ELECTRIC BOAT CO. GROTON, CONN.

Launch of the USS *Flier* at the Electric Boat Company, Groton, Connecticut. (U.S. Navy, Submarine Force Museum)

Sponsor Mrs. Anna Smith Pierce with veteran skipper Glynn "Donc" Donaho at the USS *Flier*'s launch. (U.S. Navy, Submarine Force Museum)

U.S. SUBMARINE FLIER
SPONSOR'S PARTY
LT. COM. GLYNN R. DONAHO
MRS. ANNA SMITH PIERCE
JULY 11, 1943
ELECTRIC BOAT CO. GROTON, CONN.

John Crowley, skipper of the USS *Flier*, inspects his new boat. (U.S. Navy, Submarine Force Museum)

The USS *Flier* at the Mare Island Navy Yard, April 1944. (Official U.S. Navy photo, courtesy of USS *Bowfin* Submarine Museum)

Victor John Anderson,
torpedoman's mate from
Keego Harbor, Michigan.
(Carl Anderson)

Thomas Leroy Bohn, electrician's
mate from Easton, Pennsylvania.
(Charles R. Hinman,
On Eternal Patrol Web site)

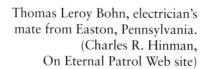

Evan Anthony Borlick,
motor machinist's mate
from Chicago.
(Charles R. Hinman,
On Eternal Patrol Web site)

Above and opposite pages:
Some of the *Flier*'s
fallen crewmen.

Charles Leon Courtright, seaman from Franklin, New Jersey. (Charles R. Hinman, On Eternal Patrol Web site)

James LeRoy, motor machinist's mate from Ely, Minnesota. (Charles R. Hinman, On Eternal Patrol Web site)

Christian John "Jack" Christensen Jr. in Australia before the *Flier*'s last patrol. (U.S. Navy, Submarine Force Museum)

Betty Thomson, winner of a "lucky legs" contest, was one of the young women in Perth who welcomed American submariners. (E. Thomson)

U.S. submarines with the tender *Pelias* at Fremantle, Western Australia. (Official U.S. Navy photo, courtesy of USS *Bowfin* Submarine Museum)

Survivors of the *Flier* on the deck of the USS *Redfin*. Standing left to right: J. W. Liddell, J. D. Crowley, A. E. Jacobson. Front row: J. D. Russo, W. B. Miller, E. R. Baumgart, A. G. Howell. Not present: D. P. Tremaine. (U.S. Navy, Submarine Force Museum)

Reunion of the *Flier* survivors fifty years later, 1994. From left to right: A. E. Jacobson, J. W. Liddell, J. D. Crowley, W. B. Miller, J. D. Russo. (A. E. Jacobson)

them as a matter of routine—perhaps because they would rather not even contemplate the possibility of ending up overboard. Another explanation is that it would have been bad for morale if only the crew on deck were wearing life preservers.[10] In any case, apart from oil, the only things that surfaced from the *Flier* were baseball-size chunks of cork. Men who came across these pieces of cork put them in their pockets for added buoyancy.[11]

Crowley had gained some notoriety at the Naval Academy for his lack of swimming ability. But fortunately for him, passing a swimming test was a requirement for graduation, and cadets who were considered below-par swimmers had to spend additional time in training and received instruction in how to survive in the water. It was a policy that probably saved many lives during the war.[12] Even so, Crowley was the oldest in the group, and he had to swim slowly, often floating so that he could rest.

Chief Charles Pope, the sonar operator, had been in the conning tower when the *Flier* went down. After about two hours in the water, Pope asked Liddell how much farther they would have to swim. Trying to sound optimistic, Liddell told him about nine miles. Pope replied, "To hell with this," and he stopped swimming. Most of the men who never made it to land simply swam silently to one side of the group, never to be seen again. The more or less calm decision to end their own lives after hours in the water was not unusual. In depositions from survivors, some of those who nearly drowned told of entering a euphoric or delirious state in which the thought of death did not distress them.[13]

Meanwhile, Liddell tried to cope with cramps in his legs. He would pinch the muscles as hard as he could to dispel the pain. Jacobson fought to keep himself awake. To cope with fatigue he constantly rotated his swimming technique, changing from sidestroke to backstroke to breaststroke. He found that his breaststroke was most effective.[14]

After four or five hours in the water, Lieutenant John Edward Casey, gunnery and torpedo officer, dropped out. He had been on the bridge at the time of the explosion, which had partially blinded him. Like Knapp, Casey had graduated from the Naval Academy in 1942, and the *Flier* was his first submarine duty. Liddell described the native of Philadelphia as "a quiet, rather tall, good-looking boy."[15] Unable to see properly or swim on his stomach, Casey frequently veered away from the group and would have to be called back. Howell was among those who assisted Casey. He stated: "I helped him until I could do no more, and then had to tell him that I was sorry but I could do nothing more. I had to watch him sink beneath the water. He put himself in God's keeping and went down without a struggle."[16] Crowley, however, believed that it had been too dark for Howell to see Casey's final moments.

At about 4:00 A.M., with the silhouette of land in sight, Crowley told the rest of the men to make their way as best they could. Unfortunately, as visibility improved, the sea became choppier. The men scattered. Gerald Francesco Madeo, the *Flier*'s helmsman, was already falling behind the main group and would be among those lost.

After fourteen hours in the water, near noon, Crowley spotted a floating palm tree and struck out for it. To his surprise, he found Liddell hanging on to the trunk. The two then spotted a larger floating palm tree, which Liddell initially mistook for a native boat. They swam for it and found three more of the *Flier*'s crew clinging to the waterlogged tree: Jacobson, Baumgart, and Howell. Baumgart, who had been reduced in rank for misbehavior while on leave in Fremantle, claimed that his determination to return and fight the charges against him provided some of his motivation for survival.[17]

The men broke off some palm fronds to use as paddles, and together they slowly pushed their makeshift raft toward shore. They were still about two miles from land, but the current helped carry them toward a reef off the southeast end of Mantangule Island.[18] As they approached the island, some of the men began to imagine that they saw houses and other signs of civilization. At about 4:00 in the afternoon the water became shallow enough for them to wade the last half mile to shore.

By the time they reached the beach, Crowley and his companions from the floating palm tree had been in the water for eighteen hours. The island was an estimated twelve miles from the site of the *Flier*'s wreck. For some perspective on their accomplishment, note that in the world of competitive long-distance swimming, any swim in open water lasting more than five hours is considered a marathon. The men of the *Flier* had survived more than three times longer, without the aid of bathing caps or suits, goggles, earplugs, sunscreen, or support crews. Even more critically, they lacked any drink or food to stave off dehydration and exhaustion. Without nourishment to replace spent energy, and without drinking water, their muscles weakened, and toxins built up in the bloodstream.[19] In addition, all five men, stripped down to their underwear, were suffering from severe sunburn, and their feet were cut and bleeding from crossing the coral reef.

To their surprise, they found James Dello Russo, now quartermaster third class, already on the island waiting for them. Miraculously, he had swum the entire distance without the aid of a palm tree or anything else. The group decided to spend the night on the narrow sand beach that stretched for about seventy-five yards at the water's edge. Several men set about building a lean-to, and Liddell hiked off to the eastern end of the island to look for water and food. He found neither, but he did encounter Donald Paul Tremaine, fire controlman second class, and guided him back to the others. Earlier, the group clinging to the palm tree had spotted Tremaine in the distance and had waved and yelled at him. Although Tremaine had waved back, he then appeared to ignore them. Tremaine later explained that he thought they were local fishermen, and if they were not friendly enough to pick him up, he thought it best to avoid them.[20] This wariness of strangers in a strange land would persist in the coming days.

12

Castaways

The survivors of the *Flier* found themselves in a situation similar to that of other shipwrecked sailors for centuries: they were isolated, hungry, and exposed to the elements. In one sense they were more fortunate than most, because among the survivors were several officers, including Commander John Crowley. Studies of sailors left adrift in lifeboats and rafts after the loss of a ship indicate that the presence of commissioned officers significantly increases the survival rate. With a respected leader, men are more confident and less likely to fall into a sense of hopelessness.[1] However, the *Flier* men also faced a distinct disadvantage: they were deep in enemy territory.

With no food or water to be found, the survivors spent their first night on the beach. All the men had severe sunburns that added to their immediate discomfort. Once the sun went down, the temperature plunged, and they faced a long, cold night dressed only in their underwear. They burrowed themselves into the sand and hugged one another to keep warm. Alvin Jacobson spent most of the night wishing the sun would come up so that he could stop shaking.[2]

The following morning they set about exploring the island, which they found to be about four miles long and mostly covered in thick shrubs. From the beach they could see the area where the *Flier* had gone down. There was no sign of life apart from an airplane spotted at about 3:00 in the afternoon. Later, however, they witnessed a strange phenomenon. According to Crowley's report, at 6:00 P.M. "a large geyser of water was seen on the general bearing of FLIER followed by the sound of a distant explosion, the source and reason for the explosion is unknown."[3] Had the submarine wreck drifted into another mine? Or did the explosion emanate from inside the *Flier*? In 1989 survivors from the Soviet submarine *Komsomolets* (K-278) would report a powerful explosion from the depths, believed to be from the detonation of its torpedoes.[4]

Only an hour earlier, Wesley Bruce Miller, motor machinist's mate third class, had arrived at the survivors' makeshift camp. Miller had landed on the western end of the island near sunset the previous day and had spent the night there. He had seen no food or water on his journey, confirming that the island could not sustain the men. The lack of water was the most immediate threat to their survival, and the tropical conditions accentuated dehydration. The pain from sunburn, sore feet, and hunger would eventually pale compared to the intensity of their thirst. Although there were cases of men lasting more than a week without fresh water, a wartime study indicates that the critical threshold for most survivors was four ounces of water per day.[5]

On a reconnaissance of the island's east coast, Crowley and Liddell found hundreds of coconuts washed up, only one of which was unspoiled. They divided the coconut among all the men, with each receiving about two tablespoons of milk and a small piece of coconut flesh barely more than an inch square. Even so, they found it impossible to keep this meager fare down.

From the eastern end of the island they could see a string of other islands: Byan, Gabung, and Bugsuk stretched toward the much larger island of Palawan. The group decided to build a raft and sail for Palawan, stopping off at the smaller islands en route. The long, narrow island of Palawan, some 270 miles long by 20 miles wide, defines the western extremity of the Philippines. It divides the South China Sea from the Sulu Sea like a breakwater. Balabac Strait lies directly to the south. Most of Palawan's

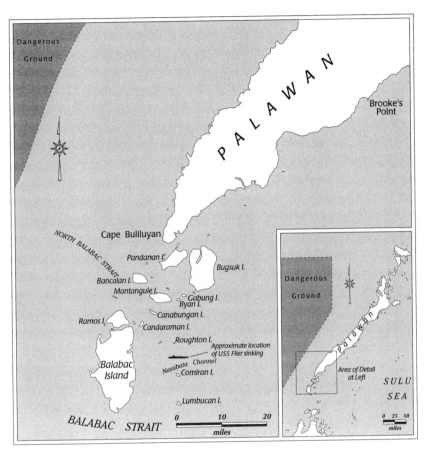

The Balabac Strait

population lived in the northeastern part of the island. With a mountain chain running for much of the island's length, communications were primitive, and travel was largely along crude tracks.[6]

Before the war, the U.S. Navy had considered establishing a base at Malampaya Sound on Palawan's east coast. The idea had been rejected for a number of reasons, including the site's exposure to naval bombardment and a narrow harbor entrance that could easily be blocked.[7] Unknown to the *Flier*'s crew, a party of coast watchers had only recently been deposited on Palawan from the submarine *Seawolf*. Departing from Darwin on 1 August 1944, the *Seawolf* carried six men under Master Sergeant Eutiquio B. Cabais, along with five tons of supplies. The party would not only provide intelligence but eventually aid in the evacuation of thirteen downed Allied airmen.[8] The coast watcher group, however, was situated in the northern part of the island, far from the *Flier* survivors' destination.

In the early afternoon of Wednesday, 16 August, the men scoured the beach and began gathering pieces of bamboo, about four inches in diameter, for the construction of a raft. Liddell and James Russo managed to wrench some vines from the jungle, and these were used to lash the bamboo together. The completed raft was approximately seven feet by four feet—anything larger would be too easily spotted by the Japanese. Arthur Howell put together two makeshift paddles, and the men also found a couple of long poles to help propel the raft.

As the work on the raft progressed, the men became weaker and less focused. They had gone two days without water. They placed about twenty seashells on the beach to collect rainwater, but although they could see squalls at sea, they barely collected a drop. At one point Howell licked the moisture off some leaves but then became violently ill.

By the following morning the raft was complete. The men decided to wait until low tide, anticipated at midafternoon, to shove off. In the meantime, Jacobson and Donald Tremaine managed to find two unopened coconuts and divided the contents among the survivors.

At about 3:00 in the afternoon they set off for Byan Island. Howell and Russo, considered to be the strongest, were designated to ride on the raft and paddle. The rest of the survivors floated in the water and clung to the raft, using their legs for propulsion. About halfway to Byan Island they spotted a Japanese plane and tried to remain as still as possible as the plane flew over. At one point there was a brief rain shower, and the men desperately tried to catch some of the raindrops in their gaping mouths. As they approached the island the current became stronger, and they seemed to be making little progress. Finally they reached the northwestern end of the island just after sunset. The men collapsed on the beach, too exhausted to even talk to one another. Again that night they buried themselves in sand against the cold, but their violent shivering caused the sand to cascade off them. Jacobson and Liddell tried to bury themselves together, but the sand only came off twice as fast. There was nothing to do but hope and pray and wait for the warmth of daylight.[9]

At dawn the next day they set off around Byan Island, reaching the far side at about 1:30 in the afternoon. At low tide they began making their way across the mile-and-a-half-wide channel to the island of Gabung. The water was shallow enough to wade part of the way, which made the journey easier. While making the crossing, however, they spotted a chilling sight—the dorsal fins of sharks cutting the water.

The terrifying prospect of shark attack loomed large in the minds of shipwrecked sailors and downed aviators during the war. Men left adrift in small boats or life rafts often told stories of sharks harassing their craft, sometimes poking their snouts over the gunwales. After the destroyer escort *England* sank a Japanese submarine off Bougainville in May 1944, the crew lowered a boat to investigate the debris. They found none of the submarine's crew but had to fight off large sharks in order to pull wreckage from the water.[10]

Fortunately, the *Flier*'s men were unmolested, and they beached at Gabung's southwest point at sunset. It was their fourth night on the islands and their fifth day without any substantial nourishment. Crowley recalled it as the "worst day yet."[11] Their arms and backs were blistered by the sun, and their feet were lacerated from walking on the coral reefs. To add to their misery, they were now beset by swarms of biting insects. Crowley began to doubt whether they could make the next three-mile crossing to Bugsuk Island.

The next day they moved along Gabung's south coast, pushing the raft ahead of them. At one point they came across a dugout canoe, but it was full of holes and useless. The search for food yielded only one edible coconut, which was again divided eight ways. From a vantage point on southeastern Gabung Island, they could see a group of buildings on adjacent Bugsuk Island. Their hopes began to soar, and they started for the island at 2:00 P.M. Because the water was shallow they were able to pole much of the way, and the crossing to Bugsuk was accomplished more quickly than expected. The wading, however, meant more damage to their feet. They landed at about 5:30 and took care to keep out of view of any possible occupants.

Once on Bugsuk, they approached the buildings cautiously. On closer inspection, it appeared that the buildings had been deserted for some time. They contained no furniture or tools, and the floors were strewn with papers. Earl Baumgart discovered a water cistern behind a house, and for the first time in almost a week, they were able to quench their thirst. There was also a grove of coconut trees, and after some effort, they managed to knock down several coconuts to eat. After this modest feast they looked for a place to sleep in one of the buildings.

Further investigation of the premises led to the conclusion that the site had once belonged to a wealthy plantation owner. There were discarded receipts for the sale of cattle and lumber, and clearings around the house had apparently been vegetable gardens at one time. The men also found a stream stocked with fish. With their dietary prospects suddenly improved, they retired in good spirits. Jacobson found a bamboo door that he used as a mattress, and for the first time since leaving the *Flier*, he slept relatively well.[12]

13

Guerrillas

At daybreak the next morning, 19 August, Alvin Jacobson was the only one up when a young Filipino man approached him, using sign language to indicate that he was friendly. Another Filipino then emerged from the jungle, and John Crowley appeared and asked them whether they were American or Japanese. One of the young men smiled and replied "Americanos." He then said "Japanese" and made a cutting motion across his throat.

When the rest of the survivors had gathered, the Filipinos explained, using their best English, that they were from a guerrilla group known as the Bugsuk Bolo Battalion. They had watched the men arrive on the island but had initially assumed they were Japanese. In fact, they had expected to find them dead, since the water cistern had been poisoned. Before leaving, the property owner had apparently laced the cistern with arsenic in order to kill any Japanese who drank from it. Although Arthur Howell had been sick during the night, his crewmates assumed that he had simply drunk too much water. The others experienced no ill effects.

The Filipinos offered to lead the Americans to their camp and supply them with food and water. As the group headed inland, they came to a sugarcane grove. The Filipinos motioned for them to sit down and then brought each man a piece of sugarcane about three feet long. Both Jacobson and Crowley would later state that this sugarcane was the best thing they had ever tasted. Typical of shipwreck survivors, they had a strong craving for sweets.[1] After about half an hour of gnawing on the sugarcane, however, they were too tired to chew anymore.

The men continued walking for about a mile, at which point they came to a building that looked like an abandoned schoolhouse. About twenty Filipinos were gathered there; four of them were armed with guns, and the rest carried spears, blowguns, and bolos (large machete-like knives). They were introduced to the Bolo Battalion leader, Pedro Sarmiento. More importantly, they were given a hot meal of rice and dried fish—their first real sustenance since escaping from the *Flier*.

Sarmiento was a former schoolteacher and plantation overseer who spoke excellent English. His group had come from Palawan in search of submarine survivors, but not survivors of the *Flier*. That was when Crowley and his crew learned that the USS *Robalo* had been lost the previous month. It appeared that some survivors from the *Robalo* had made it to Comiran Island, where they had been taken prisoner by the Japanese.[2]

Following the surrender of U.S. forces in the Philippines on 6 May 1942, various guerrilla groups began to form in the islands. These groups included both men with military backgrounds and civilians. Once news of the guerrilla movement reached General Douglas MacArthur in Australia, he sent a reconnaissance party to the Philippines under Captain Jesus A. Villamor. The thirty-nine-year-old Villamor was already a hero to the Filipinos, based on his performance as an ace pilot in the U.S. Air Corps defending Corregidor. Despite flying an outdated P-36 aircraft nicknamed the "Peashooter," Villamor had made a strong showing against the superior Japanese Zeros, and MacArthur had decorated him in the first award ceremony of the war. On 17 December 1941 Villamor had been evacuated from the Philippines on the submarine USS *Gudgeon*.

On 21 January 1943 the *Gudgeon* returned Villamor and a reconnaissance party to the Philippines, at southern Negros. The party made contact with guerrilla groups on the islands of Mindanao and Panay and helped develop an intelligence network. Villamor wielded enormous power, since he had the authority to determine which guerrilla groups would be recognized and thus receive American support. Under this scheme, the Philippine Islands were divided into ten military districts, with each district under a unified command. Eventually the guerrillas would constitute a "ghost army" in excess of 180,000 men, with more than 150 radio and weather stations.[3]

These activities were conducted under the auspices of the Allied Intelligence Bureau (AIB), founded in July 1942. A truly multinational organization, the AIB was nominally under an Australian controller, Colonel C. G. Roberts. As the director of intelligence for the Australian army, Roberts's selection to head the AIB was partly based on "diplomacy." Roberts reported to Charles A. Willoughby, who served as General MacArthur's chief intelligence officer.[4]

The connections between the U.S. submarine service and the guerrilla movement in the Philippines were close and multifaceted. At least initially, the navy was reluctant to supply submarines for AIB operations. Given the success of the submarine service in decimating Japanese shipping, any diversion from that purpose tended to be resented. According to Allison Ind, deputy controller of the AIB, the navy's attitude underwent a sudden change when it realized that AIB operatives in the Philippines could help confirm the sinking of Japanese ships. Since submarines typically headed for the depths after firing their torpedoes at enemy targets, it was often difficult to substantiate claimed "kills." A coast watcher or guerrilla with a radio, however, could verify any Japanese losses observed.[5]

Many of the arms and supplies for the guerrilla network were delivered by U.S. submarines; the first shipment landed in the Philippines on 9 July 1943. Under the direction of Vice Admiral Arthur S. "Chips" Carpender, a guerrilla supply force was formed consisting of the submarines Narwhal, Nautilus, Seawolf, and Stingray. By early 1944 the submarines were transporting an estimated 90 percent of the AIB's materials to the Philippines.[6] A former Manila attorney, Courtney A. Whitney, headed the Philippine Regional Section, which organized the submarine lifelines to the guerrillas.[7]

Initially there was no radio equipment both durable enough for jungle conditions and small enough to fit through the twenty-three-inch-diameter hatch of a submarine. Some Australian technicians managed to come up with a solution to this problem. Even before the war, Amalgamated Wireless of Australia, a government-controlled company, had pioneered the manufacture of small radio sets. It succeeded in developing a battery-powered radio that could be broken down and transported in four parts: the battery, transmitter, receiver, and collapsible antennae each fit in a waterproof metal case that was submarine-friendly. In addition to radios, submarines carried extensive propaganda material to the Philippines. Any breakable item was wrapped in newspapers proclaiming Allied victories and later circulated among the locals. A pictorial magazine titled *Free Philippines* was printed by the thousands in Australia and delivered along with cigarettes, chocolate, and chewing gum bearing MacArthur's slogan: "I shall return."[8]

Supplying guerrillas was dangerous work, and the submarines faced the inevitable risks of shallow, uncharted waters, mines, and enemy patrols. Things became even more dangerous beginning in October 1943, when American submarines became involved not only in delivering supplies but also in evacuating civilians. These evacuations became especially critical after January 1944, when the Japanese threatened to execute any Americans they found, whether military or civilian. Numerous U.S. citizens hiding out in the Philippines were transported to Australia, where they were debriefed and relocated. On 11 May 1944, for example, the USS *Crevalle* picked up twenty-eight women and children from Negros Island and dropped them off at Darwin eight days later—but not before being damaged by depth charges. Altogether, nineteen different submarines would participate in forty-one missions to the Philippines, inserting more than 300 operatives and extracting nearly 500 evacuees.[9]

Pedro Sarmiento's Bolo Battalion was only a small cog in the Philippine guerrilla movement. Compared with the organizations on some islands, the guerrillas in the region of Balabac Strait and Palawan Island were considered relatively ineffectual by the AIB. Although the Palawan guerrillas mounted an occasional ambush on a Japanese patrol, their main contribution was information gathering.

Some of the deficiencies in the region were of the Allied command's own making. As early as 10 March 1943, the Intelligence Section G-2 proposed inserting a party of coast watchers to monitor the area of Balabac Strait. Seven months later Colonel Wendell W. Fertig, the American leader of the guerrillas on Mindanao, received instructions to train a group for this purpose. A native of West Virginia and a former mining engineer, Fertig had organized a successful resistance force on Mindanao following the U.S. surrender in May 1942. The coast watchers were supposed to be picked up from Mindanao by submarine and landed in the Balabac area, but delays ensued. On 23 February 1944, when the request was finally made to insert the intelligence group on Balabac Island, the acting Seventh Fleet intelligence officer replied that there was insufficient shipping in the area to justify diverting a submarine for the mission. He also noted, prophetically, that there was a danger of mines.

Captain Arthur H. McCollum, the U.S. Navy's liaison with the AIB, disagreed. McCollum had been born in Japan and had trained in the Japanese language before heading up the Far East Section of Naval Intelligence. Contrary to his subordinate's opinion, McCollum believed that there was considerable shipping traffic in the Balabac region; furthermore, by establishing a station at Balabac Strait, they might develop contacts with guerrillas on Palawan Island. On 24 May 1944 a six-man intelligence group, led by First Sergeant Amando S. Corpus, finally left Australia on board the submarine USS *Redfin*. The *Redfin* landed the party at Ramos Island on the evening of 8 June. A rubber boat was sent in to fix a line at the beach, and the coast watchers, along with 6,500 pounds of equipment, were shuttled to their landing spot at Encampment

Point. Some weeks later, on 6 July, when their waterlogged radio equipment had finally dried out, the coast watchers established direct radio contact with Australia.[10] The same team would later play a role in reporting the fate of the *Flier* survivors.

The guerrillas on Bugsuk Island believed that a Japanese landing party was imminent. After their meal of rice and fish, the survivors of the *Flier* were hustled off in the direction of the Bugsuk River, where a sailboat was waiting. Sarmiento's instructions were to send any Allied survivors he found to the guerrilla headquarters at Cape Buliluyan on the south coast of Palawan. As a parting gift, the *Flier* men gave Sarmiento a magnifying glass from Jacobson's binoculars, which he had managed to hold on to throughout their ordeal. A grateful Sarmiento assured them that he could make good use of the gift to light his pipe.

It was a five-mile trek to the boat, and given their damaged feet and weakened condition, the submariners clearly would not be able to make the entire journey without rest. They stopped for the night at a village in the center of the island. A Filipino family graciously made room for the visitors in a small hut next to a rice paddy, and the men slept on bamboo mats.

Waking the next morning at about 6:30, the *Flier* men discovered that the generous villagers had killed a chicken to make a broth for them. They were also given some wild honey to eat. After resting for a while, they set out again. Around noontime they stopped at another hut for an hour of rest, and when they were ready to leave they were given a large basket of rice, donated at some sacrifice by the local people.

The following day they reached their destination at about 4:00 in the afternoon. The waiting sailboat was about sixteen feet long with a rounded hull. It was a type of boat used by the local Moro people, who were Muslims; they retained a distinct identity and lived mainly in the southern Philippines. A local trader, dubbed the "Sailor" by the *Flier* men, was going to navigate the boat for them. In previous navy briefings, he was precisely the type of person they had been told to avoid if they were ever shipwrecked. But the Sailor would prove to be one of the most remarkable characters they encountered on their journey. Jacobson joked that the Sailor "would be handling the tiller with one foot, rowing with the other foot, handling the sheet with his teeth, sewing up a hole in Baumgart's pants and cooking our meal, all at the same time."[11]

The party set sail down a narrow, sheltered river and had covered the three miles to its mouth by dusk. Sunset in these latitudes passed quickly; as one coast watcher put it, "You could almost hear a clunk when night fell."[12] Once at sea, the Sailor was able to negotiate the many hazardous reefs and submerged rocks despite the pitch-black night. At 3:30 in the morning they reached the guerrilla outpost at Cape Buliluyan on Palawan. Most of the men at the outpost appeared to be well educated. They explained that they would set out the following night, traveling the seventy miles to the guerrilla's main stronghold at Brooke's Point.

The next day the guerrillas rounded up some clothing for the *Flier* survivors. Each man got a pair of pants, and the lucky ones also got a shirt, although it was generally far too small. They would have to wait for footwear. Among coast watchers and guerrillas, shoes were valued above any other commodity. In the tropics, boots rotted and wore out quickly. Some of the American coast watchers resorted to wearing handmade wooden clogs whenever possible, to prolong the life of their shoes.[13]

For dinner that evening the *Flier* men had a special meal of caribou meat. It might well have doubled as shoe leather. Even though it was cut paper-thin, they found it difficult chewing.

Sergeant Pasqual de la Cruz assumed responsibility for guiding the *Flier* men to Brooke's Point. Cruz lived at Tabud in the south of the island and knew the waters of Palawan and Borneo well. He spoke a number of local dialects, and Allied intelligence considered him "thoroughly trustworthy."[14] Cruz had served in the U.S. Army Forces Far East (USAFFE), created 26 July 1941 under MacArthur's command. As the inevitability of war became clear, young Filipino volunteers had been avidly recruited, and by the end of November 1941, the USAFFE numbered more than 30,000, including 12,000 Filipino scouts. Once these forces officially surrendered on 29 May 1942, many of the recruits became guerrillas.[15]

On the afternoon of Monday, 21 August, the *Flier* men and their guerrilla escorts set sail for Brooke's Point. With favorable winds, they were optimistic about reaching their destination the next morning. They had not sailed far, however, when the Sailor turned the boat back toward the beach. In the distance they spotted a Japanese patrol boat. Once it had passed they set out again, but later that night the winds changed direction, and they ended up anchoring for the night in the Tuba River. Again a local family generously provided food and shelter.

The following day when they got under way they had two additional passengers. The family who had put them up for the night asked whether their recently married daughter and her husband might travel with them. In the early evening they encountered a group of canoes that turned out to be manned by friends of the Sailor. The canoeists provided them with fish and eel, and Russo and Baumgart decided that they would also try the local cigarettes. This proved to be a short-lived experiment, which the men likened to inhaling hot tar.

Finally, at about 8:00 A.M. on 22 August, they reached Brooke's Point, where they were greeted by a large group of guerrillas. The *Flier* men, still unable to walk well and shabbily dressed, felt self-conscious about being such poor representatives of the U.S. Navy.[16]

14

Brooke's Point

Once at Brooke's Point, the *Flier* party was taken a short distance from the beach to the home of Captain Narizidad B. Mayor, who commanded Sector D of the Sixth Military District as part of the Palawan Special Battalion. Allied intelligence was unimpressed by the organization, characterizing it as "weak, ineffectual, and badly in need of arms and supplies." Mayor was described as "not generally liked by his men who are afraid of him."[1]

Whatever his personal faults, Mayor was proud to be a representative of the U.S. military. Although a native of the Philippines, Mayor had graduated from the University of Nebraska and received a commission in the U.S. Army through the university's ROTC program. Before the war he ran a lumber business on the islands of Balabac and Bugsuk, so he knew the area well. Once the Japanese invaded Palawan, he hid his tractors and other equipment, destroyed his records, and left his home for the jungle.[2]

The Japanese had occupied Palawan's main city and port, Puerto Princesa, since early 1942. They began carving an airstrip out of the jungle, using American prisoners transported from Manila for labor. On 14 December 1944, most of the POWs would become victims of a massacre. The men were herded into air-raid trenches at the prison camp, doused in aviation fuel, and set on fire. Those trying to flee the flames were shot or bayoneted. Only 11 of the 150 men survived the atrocity. Visitors to the island after

105

an Allied invasion in 1945 still found ample evidence of the massacre: skeletons in tattered clothing, charred flesh, and leg bones sticking out of rotting boots.[3]

Apart from Puerto Princesa, located in the center of the east coast, most of Palawan Island was outside direct Japanese control. Of the approximately 2,000 Japanese soldiers on Palawan, most were stationed at Puerto Princesa under Captain Kojima Chokichi. Smaller detachments were posted at Dumaran Island to the northeast and at Conon and Pandanan islands to the southwest. For the most part, the Japanese soldiers limited their activities to seizing rice crops and making occasional patrols.

In August 1942 six U.S. servicemen managed to escape from the Puerto Princesa prison camp. The escapees—three sailors and three marines—joined a small settlement of other Americans already at Brooke's Point. It was around this nucleus of Americans that the guerrilla groups in southern Palawan initially developed. Within a short time they had organized enough men to beat back a Japanese landing party in October 1942. Most of the Americans subsequently moved to the island of Tawi Tawi. For a time the guerrillas were led by Vens T. Kerson. Although a Finn by birth, Kerson had worked as a U.S. Navy diver. Pasqual de la Cruz, who escorted the *Flier* survivors to Brooke's Point, had served as a guide and interpreter for Kerson.

In late 1943 the guerrillas on Palawan were organized as the Palawan Special Battalion of the Sixth Military District, headed by Major Pablo Muyco. At the time the *Flier* was lost, the battalion's total strength was about a thousand men. Sector D, headquartered at Brooke's Point under Captain Mayor, included four officers and eighty-two enlisted men.[4]

Fortunately for Crowley and his men, the organization at Brooke's Point included a recently arrived coast watcher group with radio equipment. This was the detachment under Sergeant Amando S. Corpus that had been landed by the USS *Redfin* less than three months earlier. Corpus, described as a multilingual American-Filipino, was a member of the U.S. Army 978th Signal Corps. He was also a most welcome sight for the men of the *Flier*. Jacobson professed that "this was the first time that we could feel completely relaxed because no matter how assuring the natives were, you still had a doubt about whether they would sell you to the Japs or something like that."[5]

The 978th Signal Services Company was activated in July 1943 to deal with secret radio communications from the Philippines. Radio operators were chosen from among the better-educated Filipinos serving with the U.S. Army in California. Colonel Courtney Whitney, as chief of the Philippine Regional Section, personally oversaw the selection of volunteers from the First and Second Filipino Infantry Regiments. In November 1943 about 200 radio operators from the company arrived in Australia from the United States. They underwent jungle training in a secret camp south of Brisbane at Beaudesert, Queensland. At Camp Tabragalba (also known as Camp X), a former cattle ranch, they honed their skills in communications, hand-to-hand combat, and survival. Most of the men were then deposited behind enemy lines by submarine. They were supposed to work with local guerrillas in the Philippines and provide radio reports to headquarters in Brisbane on Japanese forces and movements.[6]

The coast watchers at Brooke's Point had originally landed on Ramos Island, but they moved camp to Mantangule Island two weeks later. The move was precipitated by a report that there were nearly 150 Japanese troops on nearby Balabac Island, which was separated from Ramos by only a narrow channel. In addition, the locals on Ramos Island were considered untrustworthy. The coast watchers used sailboats to transport themselves and their supplies to Mantangule, arriving on 23 June.[7]

This was the same island that the *Flier* survivors had initially washed up on. But like the *Flier* crew, the coast watchers had concluded that there was no water on the island. After making contact with the guerrillas on Palawan, they relocated to Brooke's Point on 17 July. The constant humidity of the Philippines wreaked havoc with radio equipment, rotting components and shorting circuits.

Some of the coast watchers' radio equipment was inoperable when the *Flier* men arrived, but Howell was able to repair it so that they could transmit a message to Australia.[8]

On 23 August, a Wednesday, Sergeant Corpus transmitted special message number one to the commander of Task Force 71, informing him of the *Flier*'s fate: "Flier struck mine in Balabac Strait 2200?H on 13th. Sank in 30 seconds in 50 fathoms of water. Do not believe Nips know. Only eight known survivors now with P.A. at Brooke's Point, Palawan. Strong indicators that Robalo suffered same fate July 3rd."[9] The message was routed to MacArthur's General Headquarters in Brisbane, and from there to the headquarters of the Seventh Fleet. A duty officer received the dispatch at 3:00 A.M. local time on 24 August. The navy operations officer, Captain Richard H. Cruzen, was immediately notified, as was the commander of Task Force 71, Ralph Christie, in Perth.[10]

The reply sent to the coast watchers was both swift and devastating. Transmitted on 24 August, it read in part: "Why have you not forwarded information on enemy positions in South Palawan and Balabac and naval movements through Balabac Strait? Why did you not advise of presence of mines in Strait reference your Special No. 1? Your mission is to cover that area and advise me instantly of all important enemy dispositions and naval movements. Results thus far are disappointing and immediate improvement in your intelligence coverage and reports is desired and expected."[11]

Three days later, Corpus committed suicide, shooting himself in the chest with his service revolver. He left no note. Those at Brooke's Point assumed, however, that his suicide was directly related to the rebuke from Australia. They thought that he might have interpreted the message not only as criticism of his mission but also as blame for the loss of the *Flier* and the *Robalo*.

Following the death of Corpus, Sergeant Carlos S. Placido assumed command of the coast watcher group. Before enlisting in the U.S. Army the day after the attack on Pearl Harbor, Placido had run a bakery business in Laguna Beach, California. His leadership of the coast watchers was confirmed by a message on 28 August. The intelligence party under Placido would remain in operation until Allied landings at Puerto Princesa on 28 February 1945. In the interim the coast watchers provided information on southern Palawan and aided a number of escapees from the Japanese prison camp.[12]

At Brooke's Point the men from the *Flier* remained weak and ill. Captain Mayor provided the survivors with some additional clothing, but they were still barefoot. They were then taken five miles inland, toward the mountain chain that runs the length of the island. Crowley was transported on a two-wheeled cart pulled by a water buffalo, and he later recalled that the animal would stop to wallow in any mud it encountered along the way.

In the cooler weather of the mountains, the men's health quickly improved. They lodged with T. H. Edwards, an American citizen, in a bamboo house built on stilts. Edwards had married a local woman before the war and ran a business at Brooke's Point. Baumgart described him as "a God-fearing man who gave the group food, shelter and comfort."[13] All Edwards asked for in return was a pair of leather shoes once a rescue party arrived. While recuperating, the men passed the time by reading six-year-old issues of *Reader's Digest* and making things out of bamboo. After a few days of a decent diet, augmented by some medicine and rations from the coast watchers, the men of the *Flier* were ready to undertake preparations for their return to Australia.

On 26 August the *Flier* group received instructions by radio from the commander of the Seventh Fleet to begin making arrangements for an evacuation. The men were supposed to designate the appropriate pickup time, location, and security signals. They also received a dispatch from the commander of Task Force 71 at Perth, stating that there were at least two U.S. submarines in the vicinity, awaiting instructions.

The next day Crowley and the others conferred with Captain Mayor about arranging transport and getting his men's cooperation for a rendezvous. Given the weakened condition of the *Flier* survivors, it was decided that the evacuation should take place at a nearby location rather than risk a lengthy journey and possible encounter with the enemy. Although atmospheric conditions were making radio transmission difficult, Crowley submitted a rescue plan to the commander of the Seventh Fleet on the evening of 28 August; a message approving the plan was received at 1:00 A.M. the following day. The men were informed that the submarine USS *Redfin* would be in the vicinity on 30 August to pick them up. Back in Australia, though, there was still concern that the *Redfin* might be sailing into a trap.[14]

15

USS *Redfin*

The USS *Redfin* (SS-272) was one of twenty-eight submarines constructed at Manitowoc, Wisconsin, under license from the Electric Boat Company. At one stage the *Redfin* had lain side by side with the USS *Robalo,* which was also being built there. The Manitowoc yard's most distinctive engineering feat was the manner in which the submarines were launched: they were dropped sideways into Lake Michigan instead of the traditional stern-first launch into the water. From Manitowoc the submarines were floated more than 1,000 miles down the Illinois and Mississippi rivers until they reached New Orleans.[1]

After being commissioned on 31 August 1943, the *Redfin* left New Orleans for Fremantle on 15 October 1943. This was unusual, since most new submarines made their way to Pearl Harbor for their initial patrols. Only after operating out of Fremantle for a year did the *Redfin* head for Pearl Harbor as part of a wolf pack with the USS *Barbero* and the USS *Haddo.*

The *Redfin* made its first war patrol out of Fremantle on 4 January 1944, skippered by Robert Donovan King. After this patrol, on 2 March 1944, King was replaced by Lieutenant Commander Marshall Harlan "Cy" Austin. The thirty-three-year-old Austin was from Eldorado, Oklahoma, and had graduated from the Naval Academy with the class of 1935. At the academy, Austin was remembered as an avid rower and for his habit of taking a cold shower every morning. He entered the submarine service in 1940 and had been deployed in the Philippines when the Japanese attacked Pearl Harbor. At the time, his wife was back in Honolulu, only weeks away from giving birth to their first child.[2]

Under Cy Austin, the *Redfin* departed for its second war patrol on 19 March. During this patrol the *Redfin* sank two Japanese freighters as well as the destroyer *Akigumo.* The highly mobile *Akigumo* had been an escort for the Japanese forces attacking Pearl Harbor, participated in the Battle of Midway, and later helped evacuate Japanese troops from Kiska in the Aleutians. On 11 April 1944 the *Redfin* torpedoed the destroyer some thirty miles southeast of Zamboanga in the Philippines. The ship went down with 137 men, including its captain, Lieutenant Commander Atsuo Iritono.[3] This was an impressive debut for Austin's first command. The *Redfin* received credit for sinking an estimated 10,000 tons of enemy shipping, making it the most successful Fremantle-based patrol of the month.[4]

The *Redfin* began its third patrol on 26 May 1944 in the company of the USS *Harder,* commanded by Sam Dealey. The two submarines already shared an impressive history: on the same day the *Redfin* sank the *Akigumo,* the *Harder* sank the *Ikazuchi,* another Japanese destroyer. As they left Fremantle for their fifth war patrol, the *Harder* and Dealey were about to enter the realm of submarine legend. Carrying two Australian commandos, the *Harder* was headed for Borneo to rescue a group of secret operatives being pursued by the Japanese. In addition to rescuing the operatives, the *Harder* claimed the sinking of five Japanese destroyers along the way. It would be proclaimed one of the most brilliant submarine patrols of the war.

The *Redfin*'s patrol would prove highly successful as well. On their way north, the *Redfin* and the *Harder* stopped at Exmouth Gulf to refuel. In addition to its regular crew, the *Redfin* carried a small intelligence party bound for Balabac Strait—Sergeant Amando Corpus and five enlisted men, the same group that would later radio Australia and inform headquarters of the *Flier*'s fate. The commandos on board both submarines took the opportunity to train at Exmouth. Corpus and his men practiced handling their rubber boats and borrowed a manila line from the *Harder* that would later be used to help land their equipment.

Having landed Corpus and his coast watchers on Ramos Island on 8 June, the *Redfin* proceeded to carry out reconnaissance off the Japanese anchorage at Tawi Tawi. On the morning of 13 June, Austin watched as a vanguard of destroyers and two heavy cruisers departed Tawi Tawi. A couple of hours later a fleet of at least six aircraft carriers, four battleships, five heavy cruisers, and their escorts emerged from the anchorage. The submarine was unable to close on the Japanese ships or to keep up with them as they steamed off. That evening, though, the *Redfin* sent a radio message about the fleet's movement. This intelligence, combined with that of other submarines, including the *Harder,* made a substantial contribution to the American victory in what became the Battle of the Philippine Sea.

At the end of the patrol the *Redfin* radioed that it was heading back to the barn for some "moose milk"—a mixture of whiskey, Advocat liqueur, and milk. On leave, Austin and his officers had developed a reputation for drinking the strange concoction. The *Redfin* received credit for sinking two enemy ships, later confirmed by JANAC.[5]

The *Redfin* commenced its fourth war patrol when it departed Fremantle on the afternoon of 6 August 1944, along with the USS *Jack*. Eight days later the *Redfin* passed through the Malay Barrier at Lombok Strait, exchanging recognition signals with the southbound USS *Cabrilla*. By 19 August the *Redfin* was laying mines at Api Passage, replenishing a field of twenty-three mines initially laid by the USS *Trout* in April 1943.[6] Austin and his crew may have reflected on the fact that the *Trout* was now missing, having disappeared with all hands on its eleventh war patrol in February 1944.

A few days later the *Redfin* was patrolling west of the Balabac Islands. Austin was clearly aware of the danger posed by enemy mines, and on the afternoon of 22 August he noted in the patrol report, "I did not know my position very well and was afraid of the mine fields."[7] At 9:00 P.M. on 24 August the submarine received instructions to proceed to coordinates in the Sulu Sea. The *Redfin* reached its destination at about noon on 27 August, and at 6:40 that evening it was ordered to patrol the central Sulu Sea area. The *Redfin* headed east toward the atoll-like Tubbataha Reefs, located about 100 miles southeast of Puerto Princesa. The following day, near midnight, the crew received instructions for a special mission. Given the *Redfin*'s recent experience with special missions in the Palawan area—that is, landing the coast watchers on Ramos—it was an obvious choice to pick up the stranded *Flier* crewmen.

Austin's personal reaction to these orders is unknown, but most submarine commanders were less than enthusiastic about the prospect of a special mission. Many skippers resented any distraction from what they perceived as their main objective—sinking Japanese shipping. In fact, submarines on special missions were often forbidden to attack enemy ships, to avoid compromising the operation.[8]

Robert Foley, skipper of the *Gato,* complained that special missions meant not only time off station but also danger due to shallow waters and enemy ambushes.[9] These dangers were all too familiar to Austin and the *Redfin* crew. During its second patrol out of Fremantle, the *Redfin* had attempted to extract a group of Australian commandos, code-named Python, from northeastern Borneo. Harried by the Japanese and running short of food, the commandos were desperate for evacuation. The *Redfin* reached the proposed rendezvous on 2 May 1944, but when a boat party from the submarine went in to get the commandos, it was ambushed by the Japanese. The submariners were lucky to escape with their lives, and the planned evacuation was aborted.[10] These Python commandos were the same men eventually rescued in June by the *Harder.*

Memories of the aborted rescue attempt on Borneo may have dampened the *Redfin* crew's enthusiasm for a similar mission. However, the prospect of rescuing fellow submariners likely tempered their aversion to getting too close to shore.

The *Redfin* surfaced at 6:40 P.M. on 29 August, setting course to carry out its mission. The submarine was supposed to rendezvous with a "friendly boat party" at 8:00 P.M. on 30 August off Brooke's Point. Austin's orders were to pick up not only the eight *Flier* crewmen but also a British missionary and his family. If the coast was clear, three white lights would shine from the Brooke's Point lighthouse.

In the early hours of 30 August the *Redfin* made radar contact with Tagalinog Island, an eighteen-hectare dot in the ocean not far off Brooke's Point. The *Redfin* patrolled to the east, and before sunrise it dived and began navigating a course to the rendezvous point. By early afternoon the crew spotted a cargo ship heading toward Brooke's Point from the north. To their dismay, it anchored within a mile of the rendezvous coordinates. Was this an unlucky coincidence or a Japanese trap?

The *Redfin* crept to within 3,000 yards of the suspect craft. It did not appear to be armed, but it definitely carried radio equipment. The submarine watched and waited.

16

Evacuees

From shore the *Flier* survivors also watched with unease as a Japanese ship parked itself near the designated rendezvous point at 1:30 in the afternoon. Crowley and his men had arrived at the beach that morning, transported by water buffalo. Some of the men were still without shoes.

The Japanese craft was described as a small *maru,* or sea truck, of about 200 tons. The Japanese relied heavily on such small wooden cargo ships for logistical support. The sea trucks were typically distinguished by their boxlike design, and they were sometimes armed with machine guns, mortars, or a three-inch gun.[1] This particular ship did not appear to be armed, but its presence was a severe blow to the men's morale, since they assumed that the Japanese had somehow gotten wind of the rescue plan. Nevertheless, they continued to prepare for their departure.

The number of evacuees had more than doubled from the original eight survivors of the *Flier* to a total of seventeen. Included among this number were a Scottish missionary, his wife, and their son and daughter. A. M. Sutherland, described as "representing no particular faith," had lived on Palawan Island for the past twelve years. His son, Alistair, was six years old, and his daughter, Heather, was only three. Sutherland mainly looked after the health of the locals, but he also seemed to be eager to contribute to the Allied war effort. He claimed to have some knowledge of Japanese airfields on the island and the prison camp at Puerto Princesa.[2] The day after the *Flier* survivors arrived at the home of T. H. Edwards, Sutherland had paid them a visit, and at Crowley's request, the missionary conducted a religious service for them. Jacobson described Sutherland as "a fine person" and the church service as "very impressive."[3]

A number of others also waited at Brooke's Point, hoping to catch a ride to Australia on the *Redfin*. Each man had his own extraordinary story of survival in the wake of the Japanese invasion. Two of the men were from the U.S. Army. George V. Marquez and William E. Wigfield had enlisted in 1940 and were working on the ground crew at the Nichols Field air base in Manila when the war broke out. On 14 December 1941 they were evacuated to Mindoro, and after the surrender of Bataan in April 1942, Marquez, Wigfield, and about fifty others headed for the hills. They made their way to northern Panay and then sailed south in a boat. They were at Cuyo Island when the Japanese troops arrived on 20 May 1942. Most of their companions surrendered to the Japanese, but the two ex-soldiers took to the hills again. They arrived at Brooke's Point in December 1943.

Charles O. Watkins was an American sailor. He had been with the ground forces of Pat Wing 10 at Olongopo, but after evacuation he ended up with the Naval Coast Defense Battalion at Marivivalles. In March 1942 he transferred to Fort Hughes in Manila Bay, and he surrendered to the Japanese on 6 May 1942. He spent some time in Bilibid Prison at Manila and a prison camp on northern Luzon. From there Watkins endured a forced march to the Bonbabong concentration camp. Along with 350 other prisoners, he was eventually sent by freighter to the prison camp at Puerta Princesa. He escaped from that camp on 12 August 1942 and later met up with Marquez and Wigfield in northern Palawan.

Henry C. Garretson was a U.S. citizen and a civil engineer. He had worked in the Philippines since 1920, first for the government and later in business for himself. Once the war began he worked as a demolition engineer for the army and helped salvage arms and ammunition from the SS *Panay*, which had been sunk in March

1942 by Japanese planes in Campomanes Bay at the island of Negros. Divers retrieved the *Panay*'s cargo to arm the local guerrillas. In September 1942 Garretson headed south in an attempt to recruit help for the guerrillas on Panay and Negros. By the time he reached Brooke's Point he had contracted malaria. He stayed in the area and helped organize the Philippine constabulary force.

The night before the planned evacuation, Vens Kerson arrived at the Edwards home. He had been traveling the district, collecting rice to help feed the guerrillas and sometimes trading beer or whiskey salvaged from Japanese ships. Jacobson declared the forty-four-year-old Kerson to be "one of the most interesting persons I have ever met." Austin described him as a "soldier of fortune."[4] Kerson had fought the Japanese at Shanghai in 1932 and later joined the American army at Cebu after the war began. His skills included diving and, like Garretson, he had worked on the salvage of the *Panay*. After living for a time in the mountains, he traveled to Brooke's Point and, as previously noted, led the local guerrilla movement for a time. Not the least of his dangerous activities included dismantling Japanese mines that washed ashore; he then used the black powder to reload shotgun shells for the guerrillas.

To make their escape, the evacuees borrowed two boats from a local Moro described as the "District Dato." One of the boats was equipped with an outboard motor and a hand-cranked radio. There was no shortage of fuel, since it was not uncommon for fifty-gallon drums of gasoline to wash ashore from Japanese ships. There was, however, a shortage of lubricating oil, and Crowley promised to provide the Moro boat owner with some oil from the *Redfin* when it arrived. They also borrowed a portable transmitter-receiver from the coast watchers to carry in one of the boats.[5]

With the Japanese ship still sitting offshore that evening, there was no way to display the designated signal from the Brooke's Point lighthouse. The *Flier* men and the other evacuees set off in the two boats, one towing the other, at about 8:00 P.M. The plan was to go down the coast for three or four miles, carefully avoiding the anchored Japanese ship, and attempt to contact the *Redfin* by radio. Unfortunately, they got no response from the *Redfin*. They decided to keep moving southeast, taking them even farther from the Japanese ship. If they were still unable to establish radio contact, at least they could attempt a light signal. Once in position, Russo tried to signal the submarine with a shielded lamp.[6]

When they failed again to make contact with the submarine, the evacuees grew increasingly tense. Unbeknownst to them, the *Redfin* had actually received a message from the boats earlier in the evening using the designated codes, but it had been unable to establish two-way communication. At around 11:00 P.M. a discouraged Austin took the *Redfin* out to sea to charge the batteries. Back in the boats, some of the evacuees claimed that they could hear the submarine's engines, but others dismissed this as wishful thinking.

Finally, near midnight, radio contact was made using continuous-wave keying. Apparently, static from the boat's outboard motor had prevented them from establishing voice communications. By this time, the boats were five miles off Brooke's Point, and at 12:43 A.M. the *Redfin* spotted them.

As it happened, the *Redfin* was carrying two Australian commandos. Following the *Harder*'s successful use of commandos to evacuate the Python operatives from Borneo, Admiral Ralph Christie agreed to their routine presence on U.S. submarines. Designated Operation Politician, the idea was that these men might be useful in checking local sailing craft, carrying out beach reconnaissance, conducting interrogations, or attacking targets of opportunity. The policy of assigning pairs of Australian commandos to some submarines continued until May 1945.[7]

Major William Jinkins, planner and leader of the Python extraction, was now on the *Redfin*. He was assisted by Lieutenant T. J. Barnes. The pair had already made themselves useful by checking sailboats for Japanese soldiers or radios that might be used to transmit the positions of U.S. submarines. On 29 August Christie wrote to Vice Admiral Thomas Kinkaid and noted how fortunate it was that the *Redfin* was carrying Jinkins and Barnes, along with their special equipment.[8]

To ensure that there was no trap, Jinkins and Barnes paddled a low-profile canoe, known as a folboat, to the evacuees' waiting boats. Once the crowded boats were checked, the submarine pulled alongside and flooded down to take on the passengers. Austin, an old friend of Crowley's, was able to recognize his voice. Although Austin had been four years behind Crowley at the Naval Academy, in the small world of submarine skippers, most of them knew one another personally. Austin was also pleasantly surprised to recognize two of the coast watchers he had landed on Ramos Island on 8 June. The radio equipment being used had also been shipped in by the *Redfin*.[9]

By shortly after 1:00 A.M. the evacuees were on board, and the *Redfin*'s crew began off-loading arms and stores for the guerrillas. They emptied out most of the submarine's armory, including two .30-caliber Browning automatic rifles capable of firing 500 rounds a minute, two .30-caliber machine guns, two .45-caliber Thompson submachine guns, four .30-caliber Springfield rifles, three .30-caliber M-1 rifles, and ten .45-caliber Colt automatic pistols. This hardware was accompanied by nearly 26,000 rounds of ammunition.

In addition to the promised lube oil, the *Redfin* left considerable stores for the coast watchers and the guerrillas: medical supplies, food, writing materials, radio tubes, playing cards, soap, toilet paper, and 200 cartons of cigarettes. At 1:51 A.M. the coast watchers set off in the two small boats, which were now full of booty. Meanwhile, the civilians and the military evacuees who had never been on a submarine were about to enter the unnerving world of underwater travel.

17

On Board

With the stores for the guerrillas off-loaded and the passengers safely aboard, Austin decided to attack the Japanese ship that had made such a nuisance of itself. At 2:41 A.M. the *Redfin* pulled within 2,500 yards of the ship and opened fire with its four-inch and 20 mm deck guns. The four-inch gun was capable of firing thirty-three-pound high-explosive shells up to 16,000 yards; the 20 mm gun had a more modest maximum range of 4,800 yards.[1]

Sitting against the darkened landscape, the Japanese craft presented a difficult target. When the firing commenced, the ship quickly hoisted anchor and headed into shallow water. The *Redfin* gave chase but had to abandon the pursuit fifteen minutes later, after firing twenty-seven rounds from the four-inch gun and another sixty rounds of 20 mm ammunition. Although the darkness made it difficult to judge, Austin believed that they had scored no more than two or three hits on the ship. In fact, it was discovered later that shells from the submarine's four-inch gun had exploded in the surrounding hills, fortunately doing no harm to civilians.

Despite their failure to sink the ship, the new passengers seemed to enjoy the excitement. Austin noted in his report on the mission that six-year-old Alistair Sutherland had yelled "Kill the Japs!" during the entire attack.[2]

For those new to submarine transport, the experience could be exhilarating or frightening, depending on their point of view. The younger the passengers, the more quickly they seemed to acclimatize. Coast watcher Bob Stahl recalled the unnerving noises of crackling and knocking that accompanied running submerged. One of his fellow passengers suffered a black eye and abrasions after failing to get down a ladder quickly enough during a crash dive.[3] The most daunting task, however, was adapting to the stench belowdecks. A combination of fuel oil, cooking aromas, cigarette smoke, and body odor pervaded the boat. The olfactory senses eventually became numbed, but the process began anew after each exposure to fresh air. Years after leaving the service, a mere whiff of diesel fuel could transport some submariners back to their days on patrol.[4]

Most passengers were confined to the forward or after torpedo rooms, where torpedoes occupied much of the limited space. For the general safety of the craft, they were rarely allowed to move about, apart from the necessity of visiting the head, where they had to compete with the crew for the two toilet stalls. The complicated mechanisms of the head presented their own dangers, since turning the wrong valves or levers could result in blowback. Sleeping quarters usually consisted of nothing more than a hard deck, with little comfort other than a blanket. For the crew, taking on passengers could lift their morale and afforded a welcome break in the routine. Children were especially popular, and they often left the submarine wearing miniature sailor's uniforms.[5]

After the initial excitement of being rescued, the *Flier* survivors likely experienced a period of anxiety on the *Redfin*. A common reaction among wartime shipwreck survivors was an apprehension that their rescue vessels would be sunk on the return passage.[6] During the cruise back to Australia, the *Redfin*'s pharmacist's mate treated the *Flier* men for various cuts and injuries; he also put them on a course of quinine and atabrine to prevent malaria. Although Tremaine suffered from attacks of malaria, the health of the remaining survivors quickly improved.[7]

The *Redfin* made its way south through the Sibutu Strait, Bangka Strait, and Molucca Passage, arriving off Darwin in the early hours of 5 September. After exchanging recognition signals with the USS *Nautilus,* the *Redfin* moored at the main jetty at 7:40 A.M. There, the evacuees from Palawan Island parted company with the *Redfin,* and personnel from the tender USS *Coucal* began carrying out minor repairs on the submarine.

In total, almost 500 people were evacuated by submarine from the Philippines. The first large group that included civilians was transported by the oversized cruiser submarine *Narwhal* in November 1943. These operations were kept top secret, since it was feared that if the Japanese learned of the evacuation program, there would be wholesale reprisals.[8]

People evacuated from the Philippines were considered important potential sources of intelligence. From Darwin they were flown by army transport planes to Queensland. To maintain secrecy, the American Red Cross took over the small Strathalan Hotel at Caloundra, seventy miles north of Brisbane, which provided a relatively isolated locale for debriefings by G-2 and counterintelligence officers. Evacuees were usually given about a month to recover, both physically and mentally, before embarking for the United States, and Alice Thompson of the Red Cross headed the recuperation center.[9] Operations at the hotel were wound up in August 1944, so it is unclear whether the passengers from the *Redfin* ever reached this destination.

The town of Darwin's devastated appearance, the result of successive Japanese bombings, often shocked newcomers. Early in the war, the U.S. Navy had considered using Darwin as a major submarine base, but the lack of amenities and the characteristics of the harbor ruled this out. The expansive harbor was vulnerable to enemy mines, and huge tides made mooring next to a submarine tender extremely difficult. Submarine crews sometimes had to climb a tall ladder to disembark at the dock; then, on their return, they had to climb up to board the submarine. Despite these limitations, by early 1944 Darwin was an important staging base for submarines.[10] The port offered little in the way of recreational facilities, however, so crews usually made a quick turnaround, heading back to sea after taking on fuel and torpedoes.

The *Redfin* crew received a mail delivery from Perth the evening they arrived at Darwin, and they spent most of the next day relaxing. The *Coucal* supplied the crew with beer, and softball games were organized. In the early evening the wardrooms from the *Redfin* and the *Nautilus* attended a barbecue at the new submarine officers' club.

After being refueled and reloaded with torpedoes, the *Redfin* departed Darwin at 9:00 P.M. on 6 September. Austin and his crew headed for the Java Sea and continued their patrol off the south and east coasts of Celebes. The *Redfin* claimed the sinking of one tanker and damage to another in torpedo attacks. It also sank a trawler and a sampan using the deck guns. Next the crew performed "lifeguard" duties, searching for downed aviators off Balikpapan, Borneo.[11]

Australian commando Bill Jinkins remained on board, but T. J. Barnes had been replaced by another commando, Alec Chew. Only a few months earlier, Jinkins and the USS *Harder* had helped evacuate Chew and others from Borneo as the Japanese closed in on them. On the *Redfin*, Jinkins and Chew were ready for action in the event that reconnaissance of an island became necessary or a limpet mine attack was called for.[12]

The *Redfin* returned to Fremantle on 4 October 1944. Due to the "variety of passengers" it had taken on, including a couple of prisoners picked up during the second half of the patrol, Austin requested that the boat be fumigated and the mattresses renovated.[13] The fourth patrol proved to be the *Redfin*'s longest to date, with fifty-seven days at sea. It was also one of the least successful in terms of Japanese shipping sunk. Despite the claim that it had destroyed one ship at 5,100 tons, this was never confirmed by JANAC.[14]

The rescued *Flier* crew spent the night in Darwin and received some fresh clothing from the army. The following day they were flown to Perth on Admiral Christie's private plane. After a twelve-hour flight, they arrived at the airport in Perth near midnight, where they were greeted by Christie's chief of staff and a pair of captains.

Once in Perth, the *Flier* survivors were split up. John Crowley stayed at Admiral Christie's residence. James Liddell and Alvin Jacobson were given a suite of rooms in the bachelor officers' quarters. The remaining enlisted men were lodged in another part of the city.[15] According to Jacobson, they were given two days to draw some pay and obtain new clothing. All except Crowley were then flown to the inland mining town of Kalgoorlie. Jacobson observed, "The admiral did not think that it was a good idea for us to be around sailors who were going back to sea."[16] After ten days in Kalgoorlie they returned for a brief stay in Perth. Within a couple of days, Jacobson was on a plane headed for the United States.

At least some of the *Flier* men, including Crowley, reported aboard the USS *Euryale,* officially designated the *Flier*'s tender. Some nicknamed the ship the "O'Reilly," but it was also commonly known as the "Urinal."[17] Ironically, the *Flier*'s crew had never laid eyes on the ship before; the converted freighter had served at forward bases before heading to Fremantle in August 1944.

Recalling the whole episode much later, Jacobson would conclude, "Thus ended a major experience of my life."[18] For Crowley, however, the ordeal was far from over.

18

Fallout

While the *Flier* was heading toward disaster in August 1944, the crew of the *Crevalle* was heading back to Fremantle for two weeks of rest and recreation. On the last night of their leave, a ship's party was held at the Cabarita Restaurant, where, for the most part, the crew remained well behaved and sober. The *Crevalle*'s skipper, Frank Walker, led a sing-along accompanied by the Cabarita band.

That evening's conclusion contrasted sharply with the wild scene at an officers' party a week earlier. The wardrooms from four submarines, including the *Crevalle*, had gathered at Molinari's Restaurant on the outskirts of Perth. After much drinking, the submariners' Australian dates were encouraged to play an old game from the Naval Academy: the women had to change sides under the table as quickly as possible, dragging their chairs along with them. Tables were overturned, and a food fight erupted. The restaurant's owner ordered the submariners out, but many departed only after hoisting their dates above their shoulders to leave lipstick imprints on the restaurant's white ceiling.

The crew of the *Crevalle* returned to duty on 23 August and received the sobering news of the *Flier*'s loss. The *Crevalle* had transited Balabac Strait on its last three war patrols. In fact, on 6 May the submarine had sunk Japan's largest tanker, the 17,000-ton *Nisshin Maru*, in the strait. At least one *Crevalle* officer, William

Ruhe, wondered whether their own lack of incident in navigating Balabac Strait had made other submarines less vigilant in avoiding the mines known to lie on either side of the channel.[1]

On the USS *Flasher*, which was scheduled to conduct its next patrol through Balabac Strait, the tension was palpable. The *Flier* and the *Flasher* had been constructed side by side and then officially commissioned within three weeks of each other. There were many friendships between the two crews. The *Flasher*'s executive officer, Raymond Francis DuBois, had served with James Liddell earlier in the war on the USS *Snapper*. It is possible that Liddell contacted DuBois on his return to Fremantle. In any case, DuBois urged the *Flasher*'s commander, Reuben Whitaker, to get the submarine's orders altered so that it did not have to transit Balabac Strait on its next patrol. Whitaker succeeded in doing so , although Admiral Christie probably needed little persuading.[2]

The loss of the *Robalo* and the *Flier* placed Ralph Christie in a delicate position. Operational losses were, of course, inevitable. But for two submarines to be destroyed under similar circumstances in such a short time span raised the possibility of systemic problems in his organization. And the news was about to get even worse. The sinking of the USS *Harder* after a Japanese depth charge attack on 24 August brought the count to three Fremantle-based submarines lost in less than thirty days.

Back in early 1943, when four Brisbane-based submarines (*Argonaut, Amberjack, Grampus,* and *Triton*) were lost with all hands, Christie had been the first to call for a formal investigation. James "Jimmy" Fife had assumed command of the Brisbane submarine base in December 1942 while Christie was temporarily assigned to the Torpedo Station at Newport, Rhode Island. Born in Nevada on 22 January 1897, Fife had graduated from Annapolis with the class of 1918. Apart from periods of obligatory service with the battleship *Idaho* and the Bureau of Navigation, he spent most of his naval career involved with submarines. In July 1940 he was sent to Britain as a submarine observer, and he was stationed in

Manila when the Japanese attacked in 1941. With the evacuation of the Philippines, he traveled on the *Seawolf* to Darwin, then to Surabaya and Fremantle.[3]

Soon after Fife assumed command at Brisbane, a string of submarine losses occurred in the Solomon Islands. The *Argonaut*, the U.S. Navy's largest submarine, was dispatched from Pearl Harbor to Brisbane to undertake special missions. Fife directed the aging boat to attack shipping near New Britain, where it was sunk by Japanese destroyers on 10 January 1943. A U.S. bomber returning from a mission witnessed the attack, which left the *Argonaut*'s full complement of 105 men at the bottom of the sea. Having been commissioned less than a year earlier, the *Amberjack* also became a victim of Japanese antisubmarine forces on 14 February. The loss of the *Grampus* in early March remains a mystery, and the *Triton* disappeared later that same month.[4]

Christie, who returned to Australia as commander of submarines in the Southwest Pacific in early 1943, expressed reservations about Fife's methods. Fife had adopted the habit of using radio messages to direct the movements of submarines at sea. At least some skippers under Fife's command resented the practice. Part of the traditional ethos of the "silent service" was the autonomy exercised by submarine skippers once they were on station. Norvell Gardiner "Bub" Ward, executive officer of the *Gato*, cynically referred to Fife's directions from shore as a "go-here, go-there" approach.[5]

More alarmingly, Christie believed that Fife's radio traffic had allowed Japanese antisubmarine forces to home in on the U.S. boats. On 25 March 1943 Christie wrote to Fife complaining that there had been 106 radio dispatches to the *Grampus* and the *Amberjack* and that 46 of them had included reports of the submarines' positions. When Fife replied ten days later, he noted that the submarine movements he had ordered were usually short, and the locations mentioned referred to routes rather than specific positions. Nevertheless, Fife stated that he had tightened radio security and decreased the number of directions from shore.[6]

When Christie informed Admiral Arthur "Chips" Carpender

that he was planning to visit Brisbane to investigate Fife's operations personally, he received a stern rebuff. Although Fife had offered to be relieved of his command, Carpender refused. Exhibiting what Fife later described as "loyalty downward," Carpender told Fife, in effect, "if you go under, I'll go with you."[7] Later, however, Carpender did ask Christie to recommend a squadron commander who could investigate the loss of the Brisbane-based submarines. That inquiry was duly carried out by Captain Allan R. McCann.[8]

More than a decade earlier, McCann, working with Swede Momsen, had been instrumental in developing a diving bell used to rescue submariners trapped beneath the sea. McCann's investigation of Fife's command was handled with the utmost confidentiality, and only Carpender was privy to his report. Years later, McCann would finally confirm that his report had exonerated Fife. According to McCann, there was no way of knowing for sure how the submarines had been lost, and he noted ominously that some might have been victims of friendly aircraft.[9]

In all these machinations, personal politics tended to frame relations among the submarine command. Christie described Fife as one of "Lockwood's gang."[10] Fife had served as Lockwood's chief of staff at Fremantle earlier in the war, and in his own words, they "got along extremely well."[11] Fife had been directly involved in Lockwood's campaign against defective torpedoes. While based at Albany in Western Australia, he had personally supervised the tests proving that the torpedoes consistently ran deeper than set. Fife had directed the USS *Skipjack* and USS *Saury* to fire a total of eight torpedoes at a fishing net set up in Princess Royal Harbor. The resulting holes in the net provided empirical evidence that the Mark 14 torpedoes consistently hit below their set depth.[12]

Fife, like Christie, had his detractors. He lacked a reputation as a "people person," and in some ways he was the antithesis of the gregarious Charles Lockwood. A onetime heavy drinker who became a teetotaler, Fife tended to keep his own company. Pale and bespectacled, he struck many people as more the schoolteacher type than a military leader. Indeed, in 1938 Fife was appointed to head the Submarine School. As a boss he gained a reputation for giving long-winded dissertations and for being a "stickler."[13] Although most of his subordinates considered him capable, he was never popular. In a letter to Lockwood, Fife initially wrote off the submarine losses under his command as "tough luck," noting that "they can't get Japs without taking chances."[14]

For Christie, the shoe was now on the other foot. Having lost two of his own submarines under similar circumstances, Christie went into damage-control mode. On 29 August 1944, even before the *Flier* survivors were picked up by the *Redfin,* Christie wrote to Admiral Kinkaid and explained that the *Flier* had been the thirteenth U.S. submarine to transit Balabac Strait since 10 February 1944, and as recently as 10 July the *Lapon* had navigated the passage without a problem.[15]

When an inquiry into the losses of the *Robalo* and the *Flier* was subsequently appointed, some detected the hand of Lockwood and Fife in the background. But Christie was adamant that he had requested the inquiry on his own initiative. Furthermore, he insisted that the investigation be carried out by an officer unconnected with his organization who possessed submarine experience and was senior in rank to himself.[16] Subsequent events suggest that this may have been Christie's undoing.

19

Bend of the Road

The man appointed by Admiral Ernest King to investigate the losses of the *Robalo* and the *Flier* was Rear Admiral Freeland Allan Daubin. Born in Lamar, Missouri, on 6 February 1886, Daubin came from the same landlocked county as Charles Lockwood. By some freak of fate, Daubin was destined to become commander of submarines in the Atlantic, while Lockwood served as commander of submarines in the Pacific. Lockwood described Daubin as "one of his closest personal friends."[1]

Daubin initially attended the University of Missouri with the intention of studying law, but in 1905 he entered the Naval Academy. He graduated with the class of 1909 and received his first submarine command in 1913. His service during World War I included stints with the navy's Bureau of Steam Engineering, the Atlantic Fleet Submarine Force, and the chief of naval operations. Daubin attained the rank of rear admiral on 26 November 1941, and when the Japanese attacked Pearl Harbor, he commanded Submarine Squadron Four as well as the submarine base at Pearl. In March 1942 he became commander of submarines, Atlantic Fleet.

Compared with the war in the Pacific, U.S. submarines played a relatively minor role in the Atlantic. Only 112 of the total 1,682 patrols carried out by U.S. submarines during the war were in the Atlantic, a ratio of one to fifteen. The submarine command in the

Atlantic served mainly to train crews and shake down new boats before they were dispatched to the Pacific. German U-boats dominated Allied strategies in the Atlantic; not until after the war were submarines regarded as an important counterweapon to enemy subs.[2]

On 8 September 1944, while en route to the forward base at Majuro in the Marshall Islands, Lockwood wrote to Daubin, filling him in on the new base at Apra Harbor on Guam and noting that submarines continued to get "nice bags" in Luzon Strait and the Yellow Sea. Lockwood closed the letter with the news that, although not yet announced, the submarines *Robalo* and *Flier* had been reported lost due to mines.[3] Ironically, Daubin was already on his way to Australia to investigate those very losses.

When Daubin arrived in Perth on about 12 September, he was initially lodged at the Weld Club. The exclusive men's club, founded in 1871, was named for former Western Australian governor Frederick Aloysius Weld. The spacious two-story brick building still occupies a premium location at the corner of Barrack Street and The Esplanade. The veranda and front windows provide views of the adjacent Supreme Court gardens and the Swan River. Inside, the ambience is one of mahogany and chandeliers, plush armchairs, card rooms, and fine dining. In the 1940s the all-male membership spent much of their time smoking cigars, drinking French wines, and playing billiards.[4]

With the outbreak of World War II, many of the Weld Club regulars enlisted in the Australian armed forces, leaving both its membership and its finances depleted. The loss of membership fees, along with wartime austerity, put pressure on the club's amenities and its shrinking menu. In an attempt to strengthen its finances, the Weld Club began extending honorary memberships to visiting American officers. Similar arrangements were made by exclusive clubs in other Australian cities, such as Tattersall's in Brisbane.[5] An occasional enlisted man managed to penetrate the sanctity of the Weld Club. According to one bit of club lore, an American sailor was discovered in the early-morning hours having sex with a woman on the tiger skin that graced the tiled foyer.

In April 1943 the Weld Club hosted Admiral Ralph Christie and his senior staff at a luncheon. Christie apparently found the notion of a club too British for his taste and rarely visited its premises. Daubin was similarly unimpressed. Even at age fifty-eight, he considered himself out of step with the Weld Club's aging residents, the oldest of whom was a veteran of the Boer War. A former club president, the man was prone to imagining that he was driving a horse-drawn carriage while sitting in bed, calling out horses by name and cracking an invisible whip over his head.[6] On top of this, there was a critical shortage of bathrooms and hot water at the club. Within a couple of days Daubin begged Christie to find him alternative accommodations.

Christie had originally viewed putting up Daubin at his own residence, Bend of the Road, as rather like "entertaining the judge."[7] Nevertheless, Christie found Daubin a place to stay by pushing his chief of staff, P. G. Nichols, into a smaller bedroom.[8] Located at 4 Crawley Avenue in the salubrious riverside suburb of Crawley, the Bend of the Road residence was owned by one of Western Australia's most intriguing women. Born in 1900 at Kalgoorlie, Alice Mary Cummins completed a law degree at the University of Adelaide and became the first woman admitted to the Western Australian bar. In 1936 she succeeded her father as the managing director of the Kalgoorlie Brewery and its affiliated hotels. A truly Renaissance woman, her interests included playing the cello, making elaborate models of Spanish galleons, and experimenting with radio transmission. When she died suddenly of a heart attack in June 1943, the obituary in the *West Australian* newspaper noted, "Of a kindly, but very retiring nature, she did many charitable deeds in a quiet way."[9] One of her acts of philanthropy had been to make her luxuriously appointed home available to the U.S. Navy a year earlier. She had long since retreated inland to Kalgoorlie, believing a Japanese invasion to be imminent.

Today the Bend of the Road site is occupied by a twelve-story luxury apartment. Although the views are now somewhat obscured by other high-rise residential units, Christie enjoyed a panoramic view of Matilda Bay and an expanse of the Swan River across to South Perth. A hundred yards to the rear, up a gently sloping hill, the street ended at King's Park, where the bush was thick with the sounds of magpies and parrots. One might suspect that part of Christie's reluctance to house Daubin at Bend of the Road was prompted by a desire to protect his privacy and his privileged lifestyle. Christie was waited on by stewards who had survived the sinking of the USS *Houston*. He also had a Packard car at his disposal, along with a personal driver, a young Dutch woman who had escaped to Perth from Java.[10]

Whereas gambling was forbidden at the Weld Club, it was an integral part of Christie's social life. By his own admission, Christie loved to gamble. He and his staff would bet on games of darts before dinner each night. Christie would play golf three or four times a week, inevitably wagering on the outcome. There were also regular poker games and shooting craps with skippers who were returning from patrols. The latter led to some resentment toward Christie. Lawson "Red" Ramage and Robert "Dusty" Dornin accused Christie of taking advantage of the skippers, getting them drunk on martinis and then taking their money at cards.[11]

Christie would later claim that Daubin's inquiry in Perth absolved his operation of any blame and actually worked to his advantage.[12] Subsequent events, though, cast some doubt on this claim.

20

Inquiry

Even at the time, the terms and objectives of Daubin's inquiry were a matter of some confusion. In hindsight, Christie's chief of staff, Philip "P. G." Nichols, was unsure whether it had been a board of investigation or a court of inquiry. Christie described it as the latter, but Herb Andrews remembered it as the former.[1] A court of inquiry was the normal means of looking into the loss of a ship, but Daubin's activities could more accurately be described under navy regulations as an investigation by one officer.

Naval discipline and penalties were set out in the colorfully phrased *Articles for the Government of the United States Navy*, popularly known as the "Rocks and Shoals." There was no independent naval judiciary, and the Uniform Code of Military Justice did not exist until 1951. Under the *Articles*, courts of inquiry could summon witnesses and punish contempt in the same way as a court-martial. However, they were empowered only to determine the facts; they did not render an opinion unless instructed to do so in the order convening the inquiry.[2] Like McCann's investigation of the submarines lost under Fife at Brisbane, Daubin's findings would remain strictly confidential.

John Crowley found his command of the *Flier* under close scrutiny for the second time. Whereas Crowley had declined representation during the investigation into the *Flier*'s grounding at Midway, this time he availed himself of the right to counsel. He chose Herb Andrews, skipper of the *Gurnard,* as his adviser. Andrews had graduated from the Naval Academy with the class of 1930, making him a contemporary of such luminaries as Dudley "Mush" Morton, Wreford "Moon" Chapple, and Sam Dealey. Finding duty on surface ships fairly unexciting, Andrews turned to submarines. He married his high school sweetheart and settled down at New London, not far from his parents' home in New Haven, Connecticut.

Earlier in the war, Andrews had worked on Daubin's staff in the Atlantic theater. He did not care much for Daubin, characterizing him as "old school." Andrews conspired to get back to sea as soon as possible, and in 1942 he was given command of the USS *Gurnard.* Andrews proved to be an aggressive skipper. On a patrol out of Pearl Harbor during April–June 1943, the *Gurnard* attacked a seven-ship convoy, firing six torpedoes for clean hits. The submarine received credit for sinking five of the ships and earned a Presidential Unit Citation. They later sank a large tanker on the same patrol.[3]

The *Gurnard* had originally been ordered to pick up the *Flier* survivors from Palawan Island, but for reasons that were unclear to Andrews, these orders were countermanded, and the *Redfin* was sent on the mission instead.[4] It is likely that the *Redfin*'s recent experience landing coast watchers in the region—negotiating the shallow water of North Balabac Strait without incident in June 1944—was considered advantageous.[5] As previously noted, the *Redfin* also had a pair of Australian commandos on board to help with the evacuation.

Crowley first approached Andrews about representing him on a late Sunday afternoon. Andrews recalled being seated in the bathtub at the time (it was not uncommon for submariners returning from patrols to spend much of their recovery time in a bathtub or shower). He agreed to assist Crowley as counsel, but there was little time for preparation, since the inquiry was scheduled to begin the next morning. Andrews asked to see Daubin's precept for the inquiry. He believed that it was important to know whether Daubin's purpose was to simply find out what had happened or to establish guilt. He did not find Daubin's response comforting. According to Andrews, Daubin stated that he had been sent by Admiral King and did not have to disclose the precept. Furthermore, since Crowley had lost his ship, he was a defendant in the inquiry.[6] Christie would later describe Daubin's interrogation of the surviving *Flier* officers as "brutal," and he "objected strongly" to the manner of questioning.[7]

Christie also saw himself as a defendant in the inquiry, or at least an "interested party."[8] He was extremely keen to get his thoughts on the record and to defend the procedures used in framing the operational orders of submarines under his command. In a letter to Admiral Kinkaid dated 29 August 1944, Christie had already outlined the rationale for assigning submarines different routes to and from their patrol areas: he wanted to avoid a "beaten path" that might be exploited by the enemy. In addition, since the *Flier* and the *Muskallunge* had departed Fremantle at the same time, having them take different routes increased the possibility of contact with enemy ships. When prescribing routes, he stated, there were a number of other factors to consider as well, including Japanese shipping movements and phases of the moon. Finally, Christie noted that since March 1943, the pass at Balabac had been used forty times.[9]

In a prepared written statement to Daubin, Christie observed that when planning operations, "in each case, the hazards are calculated against the opportunity of inflicting damage upon the enemy." He further defended the Operations Division, writing, "I do not know any better men in the submarine service for the job of Operations Officer than Captain Tichenor and Captain McLean."[10] He added that both men, like himself, had submarine combat experience.

In fact, the operational orders for both the *Robalo* and the *Flier* had been prepared by Heber Hampton "Tex" McLean because, at the time, Murray Tichenor (McLean's brother-in-law) had been on patrol with the USS *Harder*. Earlier in the war, while serving as op-

erations officer under Charles Lockwood, McLean became the first
senior officer to accompany a submarine war patrol.[11] In a sense,
Tichenor was carrying on that tradition, and as it happened, he
would be present on one of the most legendary submarine patrols of
the war: the *Harder*'s highly successful fifth patrol (see chapter 15).

McLean had served in various posts under both Lockwood
and Christie, including as Christie's chief of staff. After a stint at
Pearl Harbor, McLean returned to Christie's command.[12] He had
a reputation as a hard worker. In Perth, McLean described the
routine as working all day in the office, some darts and dinner
at Bend of the Road in the evening, followed by another stint at
the office. But it was not all work. According to skipper Wreford
"Moon" Chapple, McLean would frequently throw dockside parties for returning submarine crews and then go off with the officers
to "get boiled."[13]

It is probable that Mark Jensen, as assistant operations officer, was also involved in framing the *Flier*'s orders. Jensen had
been on the USS *Puffer*, which survived one of the most terrifying
depth charge attacks of the Pacific war. While patrolling Makassar
Strait in October 1943, the *Puffer* had been forced to remain submerged for thirty-one hours, and many of the crew cracked under
the strain. Following the incident, Jensen was transferred from the
Puffer and assigned to assist Tichenor. Nichols considered Jensen
competent, but he also believed that Jensen was still affected by his
experience on the *Puffer*.[14]

According to Christie, the orders warned of mines and underwater obstructions in Balabac Strait north of Mangsee Island.
They also included the route previously used by the USS *Crevalle*
to transit Balabac Strait.[15] Later, however, Crowley would claim
that, prior to the *Flier*'s sinking, it was not known that Balabac
Strait was mined.[16]

In his statement to Daubin, Christie defended Crowley as well
as the *Robalo*'s commander, Manning Kimmel. He declared both
men to be "officers of the highest type, professionally competent,
experienced and possessing qualities of leadership and character
that are exemplary."[17] It is clear, however, that Christie believed

that the *Flier* disaster resulted from circumstances at sea rather than its operational orders. Even before Crowley and his rescued crew returned to Fremantle, Christie speculated that the *Flier* "may very probably have been forced into shallow and mineable waters."[18] Years later, Christie continued to believe that Crowley had strayed into shallow waters. In a 1972 letter to submarine historian Clay Blair, Christie wrote that in spite of "very poor weather condition and somewhat doubtful position, he took a chance to intercept the enemy, transited Balabac out of the safe channel and in forty fathoms was mined."[19]

Just how deep the water had to be to avoid mines was a matter of contention. Slade Cutter recalled being told to stay outside the 600-fathom curve whenever possible to avoid mines.[20] In a letter to Thomas Kinkaid after the loss of the *Robalo* and the *Flier*, Lockwood conceded, "It looks as though the Nips are getting smarter with their mine activities, and we will have to be more cautious in future."[21]

The extent of Crowley's responsibility for the *Flier* disaster hinged on navigation. Had the *Flier* strayed out of the deep-water channel and hit a mine? Or had the Japanese succeeded in sinking the *Flier* with a deep-water mine in the channel? These questions cannot be answered definitively until the site of the *Flier* wreck is verified. In the meantime, a case can be made for both scenarios.

An October 1943 study by Lieutenant K. L. Veth, the Seventh Fleet's mining expert, along with an April 1944 report by a Lieutenant Suddath, indicate that Nasubata Channel could not be effectively mined. However, the same reports warned of the dangerous tidal stream and surface current.[22] Given the overcast conditions and the lack of navigational aids, it is possible that the *Flier* was swept off course. Likewise, strong currents and the inability to take star sightings were largely responsible for the *Darter*'s undoing. Although the current had been miscalculated by only a quarter knot, the *Darter* was seven miles off course when it slammed into Bombay Shoal off the west coast of Palawan.[23]

Even if it could be proved that the *Flier* had sunk as a result of navigational errors, it is doubtful that Crowley would have been formally sanctioned. When the *Darter* grounded in October, the resulting inquiry did not find its skipper, David Hayward Mc-Clintock, at fault. According to Christie, McClintock had merely tried to run down a Japanese target in dangerous waters and paid the price for his bravado.[24] The Dutch submarine *O-19* would experience a similar predicament when it grounded on Ladd Reef in the same waters. Even though the Dutch skipper, Van Hooff, conceded that he had made a mistake in plotting the submarine's course, the incident did not prove terminal for his career.[25]

Of the nearly 400 ships lost during World War II, only one captain would be court-martialed for losing his ship due to an act of war. He was Charles B. McVay III, skipper of the ill-fated USS *Indianapolis*, sunk by a Japanese submarine in August 1945. On 13 August, exactly a year after the *Flier* went down in Balabac Strait, a court of inquiry convened on Guam to consider McVay's culpability. Skipper Glynn "Donc" Donaho, who had delivered the keynote address at the *Flier*'s launching, played a role in the proceedings. He testified that even if McVay had plotted a zigzag course, it would have been of little use in avoiding the attack by the Japanese submarine. Nevertheless, the court of inquiry recommended that McVay face court-martial, a decision confirmed by Admiral Ernest King and Secretary of the Navy James Forrestal.[26]

At the time of the *Flier*'s loss, no skipper had faced court-martial under similar circumstances. Even so, Crowley had good reason to fear that his career as a submarine commander might be over. The captain was ultimately responsible for the loss of a ship, even if he was not directly at fault. Following the sinking of the submarine USS *Squalus* during training exercises on 23 May 1939, a court of inquiry found that a faulty main engine induction valve was to blame. Despite being praised for his efforts to save many of the crew, skipper Oliver Naquin would never command another submarine. Even after the outbreak of war, Naquin would serve only on surface ships.[27]

Crowley's career withstood this second formal inquiry, and he would eventually receive another submarine command. With the expanding submarine war, qualified skippers were in demand, and they were unlikely to see their careers ended prematurely. Whereas nearly a third of American submarine skippers were replaced during the first year of the war, the ratio later fell to one in seven.[28] Daubin's investigation would take its toll, however.

21

Report Incognito

Admiral Freeland Daubin departed Perth on 21 September 1944, flying on Australian National Airlines. The precise content of Daubin's report on his inquiries at Fremantle remains a mystery. Under the terms of the investigation, he reported solely and confidentially to Admiral Ernest J. King. No extant copy of Daubin's report can be located at the National Archives, Library of Congress, Naval Historical Center, Naval War College, or Office of the Judge Advocate General. Everything currently known about the report's substance is secondhand.

Admiral Ralph Christie would later claim, "Daubin had nothing but praise for the way we conducted our operations." P. G. Nichols, his chief of staff, also recalled receiving "a clean bill of health," though he conceded that neither he nor Christie actually saw the report.[1] Nevertheless, Christie would later go even further and claim that Daubin's investigation worked to his advantage, stating that he had received not only "complete exoneration" but also a "strong commendation."[2] Christie certainly used the investigation as an opportunity to beat his own drum. In a written statement submitted to Daubin, Christie emphasized the enemy ship tonnage sunk under his command, claiming that Fremantle-based Task Force 71 ran more patrols and sank more ships than its Task Force 72 counterpart in Brisbane.[3]

In contrast, Herb Andrews, acting as counsel for John Crow-

147

ley, got the impression that Daubin had been trying to develop a case against Christie. Daubin's line of questioning, he believed, suggested that Christie had been negligent in assigning routes to the submarines under his command. Andrews even got the idea that Daubin might be after Christie's job.[4] These views, however, may have been formed in hindsight after a chance encounter with "Dusty" Dornin about six months later.

Robert E. "Dusty" Dornin was one of the legends of the submarine service. Originally from San Francisco, he had been an all-American football player at the Naval Academy, graduating with the class of 1935. Slade Cutter would later recall Dornin as a hard worker at the academy who "studied all the time." Despite the distractions of sports and young women, Dornin finished near the top 10 percent of his class.[5]

After the Japanese attack on Pearl Harbor, Dornin served on the first U.S. submarine patrol of the Pacific war. Only four days after the attack, the USS *Gudgeon* departed Pearl under Lieutenant Commander Elton "Joe" Grenfell. Dornin was the submarine's fire control officer, operating the all-important torpedo data computer. On 27 January 1942 the *Gudgeon* sank the Japanese submarine *I-173* some 200 miles west of Midway. It was the first enemy ship of the war sunk by an American submarine.[6]

Dornin would go on to serve as the *Gudgeon*'s executive officer and then to command the USS *Trigger*. But after making nine submarine war patrols, his career would change course. Admiral King, chief of naval operations, wanted a successful submarine skipper as his aide. A number of the submarine service's outstanding talents would be drafted into administrative posts, causing Charles Lockwood to lament, "Possibly after we get the entire Navy manned by submarine personnel we will be allowed to retain a few of our good men."[7]

Admiral King, designated commander in chief of the U.S. Fleet on 20 December 1941, certainly had an acute appreciation of the submarine service. Although he never formally qualified as a submariner, he assumed command of Submarine Division Eleven in 1922 and commanded the submarine base at New London from 1923 to 1926. King had even submitted a design for the submarine insignia, influencing the twin-dolphin motif adopted in 1924. In September 1943 he visited Pearl Harbor and Midway, getting a firsthand look at submarines operating in the Pacific. King was a great admirer of the service, crediting submarines with sinking more than half the Japanese shipping lost during the war. It was U.S. submarines, he acknowledged, that made it difficult for the enemy to reinforce and consolidate its forward positions.[8]

Some claimed that King had an ulterior motive in seeking an unmarried submariner as his aide: King had six daughters, so a bachelor aide might prove to be a useful escort. This story seems dubious, however, since one of King's daughters was married as early as 1927, and the youngest, Mildred, had already tied the knot in September 1942.[9] In any case, Dornin was initially unenthusiastic about the appointment. Admiral Chester Nimitz tried to induce Dornin to accept the job by telling him that there were probably 700 women for every man in Washington, D.C. What neither King nor Nimitz knew, however, was that Dornin was already secretly married. Following a number of double-dates with Ned Beach, his *Trigger* executive officer, Dornin had married a young woman named Ellie.[10]

When Herb Andrews encountered Dusty Dornin at Guam some six months after Daubin's investigation, he got Dornin's version of events from inside Admiral King's office. King was well known for his quick temper and lack of patience, and one of his daughters sarcastically described him as the most even-tempered man in the navy—"always in a rage."[11] A frustrated Brigadier General Dwight Eisenhower once dubbed King a "mental bully" and declared that if someone shot him, it "might help win this war."[12] According to Dornin, after receiving Daubin's report, King complained that he had sent Daubin out to get the facts—not to get into a "pissing contest" with Christie. King allegedly stated, "I ought to order both out of their jobs."[13]

King's comments were, of course, off the record and therefore impossible to verify. But despite having more than 3 million men under his command, King was not averse to becoming personally involved in sorting out personnel matters. He was a strong believer in the tenet that when something went wrong, someone should be held accountable. For example, King personally intervened to ensure that the skipper of the USS *Queenfish,* Charles E. Loughlin, faced a court-martial after he mistakenly torpedoed a Japanese ship that had been given clearance to carry supplies for American prisoners of war. And King later overrode the recommendations of admirals Nimitz and Spruance, insisting on the court-martial of Charles McVay following the loss of the USS *Indianapolis.*

At the time, however, King may have had bigger fish to fry than Christie and Daubin. In October 1944 King received the report from the court of inquiry investigating the attack on Pearl Harbor. After the Japanese attack, Husband Kimmel had been summarily removed as commander in chief of the U.S. Fleet and forced into retirement. King had long believed that Kimmel was merely a scapegoat to assuage the popular outrage caused by the attack.[14] The debacle over the loss of the *Flier* was small beer by comparison. In King's personal memoirs, neither Christie nor Daubin rated a mention.

Regardless of whether King had a hand in events, both Christie and Daubin would be out of their jobs by the end of the year. Both men were appointed commandants of navy yards, typically regarded as the last posting for rear admirals before their retirement. In mid-November 1944, Admiral Louis E. Denfeld informed Lockwood that orders had been issued to relieve Daubin as commander of submarines in the Atlantic and make him commandant of the New York Navy Yard.[15] Daubin remained in that post until December 1945, when, following administrative reorganization, he became commandant of the New York Naval Base.[16]

For Christie, the news that he was being replaced as the commander of submarines, Southwest Pacific, came as a shock. Even worse, his successor would be his old adversary James Fife. Although Christie accepted his appointment as commandant of the Puget Sound Navy Yard at Bremerton, Washington, reluctantly, he would later put a positive spin on it. Christie cast himself as a troubleshooter charged with lifting the morale and production of the 36,000 civil employees under his authority. The posting did, in fact, suit Christie's talent for efficiency and public relations. He remained at Bremerton for three years.[17]

Precisely why Christie lost his command at Fremantle remains debatable. It is possible that he was simply caught up in the general reshuffling of positions by the Bureau of Personnel at the end of 1944.[18] Most commentators, however, perceived a darker purpose. According to Christie, in a conversation with Admiral Edwards, former commander of Submarine Squadron Two, about why he had been relieved, Edwards "evaded" his questions. Christie linked his detachment to a quarrel with Admiral Thomas C. Kinkaid over a Medal of Honor for Sam Dealey, skipper of the *Harder*. Christie had nominated Dealey for the nation's highest combat award after his highly successful fifth patrol, but Kinkaid had knocked back the recommendation, partly on the grounds that General Douglas MacArthur had already awarded Dealey a Distinguished Service Cross. Kinkaid apparently took offense at Christie's persistence in the matter.[19]

Christie's version of events is supported in some respects by Fife, who had joined Admiral King's planning staff in Washington, D.C., in March 1944. In early November 1944, personnel in Washington became aware of "a rather insubordinate message" from Christie to Kinkaid involving the latter's rejection of the former's recommendation of Dealey for a Medal of Honor. Fife suspected Kinkaid of asking that Christie be relieved of his command. In any case, a few days later, King informed Fife that he would be sent back to command submarines in the Southwest Pacific.[20]

Some believe that the loss of the *Robalo* and the *Flier* also contributed to Christie's transfer. There are even claims that in the case of the *Robalo*, Kinkaid had personal reasons for going after Christie: Manning Kimmel, the *Robalo*'s commander, was Kinkaid's nephew. After the loss of the *Robalo* and the *Flier*, Lockwood wrote to Kinkaid to express his sympathy, noting, "I know how deeply you are personally concerned."[21]

The relationship between Kinkaid and Kimmel serves as a reminder of the strong family networks within the navy—and within
the submarine service in particular. In the upper echelons, the sons
of admirals often followed the career paths of their fathers. These
family ties could be an important aspect of the often harsh politics
of command. So it is plausible that Kimmel's death played a role in
Christie's downfall. What is certain is that the loss of the *Robalo*
and the *Flier* left a wake of grief and despair.

22

Back in the USA

Before leaving for the United States, John Crowley traveled to Brisbane on 26 September to give a firsthand account of his evacuation from Palawan to the Seventh Fleet command.[1] Along with executive officer James Liddell, Crowley was also debriefed at Pearl Harbor in early October 1944. Each man was interviewed about the *Flier*'s two war patrols, and a verbatim transcript was made of their comments.

There are few clues as to how the loss of the *Flier* affected Crowley. Even during a routine war patrol, submarine commanders were under enormous stress. Decorated skipper Slade Cutter recalled having severe stomach trouble on his patrols and sleeping only a couple of hours a day while in enemy waters. He would drink up to thirty cups of coffee a day and smoke heavily to keep going, no doubt aggravating his stomach problems. A sense of responsibility for the submarine was frequently accentuated by letters from the crew's family, pleading with the skipper to bring their loved ones home alive.[2]

Before his assignment to the *Flier*, Crowley had experienced the extreme conditions of the Aleutians, where the climate, isolation, and boredom could take a heavy toll on mental health. Cases of clinical depression were endemic among servicemen there; one military physician claimed that any man who spent more than six months in the region developed a vacant "Aleutian stare."[3] Some submariners did not realize how badly they were affected by the stress of war patrols; only after extended periods of leave did they become fully aware of their mental states. Some, for instance, were afflicted with nightmares years after their service; others developed a lifelong aversion to loud noises.[4]

Psychiatric studies of World War II veterans indicate that although men could be hardened by situational stress, they could also be broken by it. During the war itself, however, there was little appreciation of how war survivors reacted to traumatic events. The diagnosis of post-traumatic stress disorder was not fully recognized by the American Psychiatric Association until 1980.[5] In part, reactions to stress and trauma are culturally determined. Whether the combatants of World War II responded to the horrors of war in the same way as Vietnam veterans, for example, is debatable. Reactions to combat stress among World War II veterans were most often characterized by emotional reticence and repression.[6]

It is possible that Admiral Daubin's inquiry in Perth helped Crowley to process and cope with the *Flier*'s loss. As a rite of passage, the inquiry marked a moving on from the disaster, especially since it apparently absolved Crowley of any blame. Psychiatric studies of veterans suggest that the morale and performance of the unit play an important role in maintaining mental health. Crowley took obvious pride in the *Flier*'s achievements on its first war patrol, and the status of the submarine service as an all-volunteer elite force within the navy may have played a significant role in maintaining sanity under extreme conditions.[7] In any case, Crowley and his comrades showed remarkable resilience. Only one of the *Flier* survivors required medical treatment for trauma after their return to the United States, and they all apparently made quick recoveries.[8]

On 11 October 1944, Crowley reported for temporary duty at the Bureau of Naval Personnel in Washington, D.C.—or BuPers, as it was generally referred to. Liddell was also assigned to temporary duty at the bureau, which was situated on a small hill near both the Pentagon and Arlington National Cemetery. It is likely that their main responsibility was to verify the men lost on the *Flier* and write to their families. The general practice, according to Charles Lockwood, was for the navy to write to the families of missing submarine crewmen "only after the loss has been admitted."[9] Even then, the official details released were likely to be extremely sketchy, and the men's relatives were advised to maintain secrecy for security reasons.

Perhaps corresponding with the relatives of his men helped Crowley come to terms with the disaster and assuage any guilt he felt as a survivor. Yet the task of writing to relatives about the death of their loved ones was no doubt a painful process. When rescue efforts failed to save the crew of the *S-4* after it sank, Swede Momsen was left to answer the queries of relatives. He recalled this as the worst time of his career: "I almost quit then."[10]

Alvin Jacobson's parents in Grand Haven, Michigan, were among the fortunate ones. They received a letter dated 14 September and signed by Assistant Chief of Naval Personnel L. E. Denfeld informing them that their son was "safe and well." At the same time, they were advised to "not divulge any reports that may come to you concerning his experiences, or disclose the name of the ship in which he served."[11]

After a brief stay in Western Australia, Jacobson was flown back to the United States on a Pan Am Clipper. The Clipper flight, with its china-service meals and sleeping bunks, was a rare bit of luxury against the backdrop of a savage war. Entitled to thirty days' survivor's leave, Jacobson spent the time with his family. Although given his choice of assignments within the navy, he unhesitatingly opted to stay with the submarine service—a powerful commentary on the comradeship forged among the men of the service, partly as a result of the extraordinary dangers they faced. At the end of November 1944 Jacobson reported to the Boston Navy Yard and became part of the crew of the newly constructed submarine the USS *Ling*. He had no idea where his seven fellow survivors were sent.[12]

Once the *Flier*'s loss became a matter of public record, the surviving members of the crew at last received some recognition. All eight survivors received the Purple Heart, and on 26 October

1944 Crowley was presented with a Navy Cross by the assistant secretary of the navy for air, Artemus L. Gates. The Navy Cross citation praised Crowley's "extraordinary heroism" and "gallant leadership" during the *Flier*'s first patrol. Liddell received a Silver Star at the same ceremony.[13] The ceremonies lent a sense of finality to the *Flier*'s loss, but one that could not be shared by the families of the dead.

23

Next of Kin

For the families of the *Flier*'s deceased crew, there was initially a roller coaster of misinformation and false hope. The *New York Times* reported the loss of the *Flier* on 20 September 1944, stating that "apparently there was no loss of life aboard the submarine." The article speculated that the *Flier*'s crew "might have been picked up by other American craft." When the *Washington Post* reported the loss of the *Flier* on 29 September 1944, it claimed that "the skipper and probably some if not all of the officers and crew of the *Flier* are safe." The *Post* made this assumption on very slender grounds, noting that although the navy had declined to respond to inquiries, it had indicated that "the next of kin of the officers and crew have been informed." To the *Post*, this phraseology, contrary to the usual statement that "next of kin of casualties have been notified," suggested that most of the men on the *Flier* had survived.

By 13 September the navy's Casualties and Allotments Section had drafted a letter to the next of kin, although it is unclear whether these letters were intended for the relatives of all the *Flier*'s crew or only those of the eight survivors. However, the letter stated in part, "He is safe, and it is likely that he will correspond with you in the near future." The letter also admonished the recipients to keep the information confidential, for security reasons.[1] By 10 October the situation for the families of those missing in action had been clarified. The commander of Submarine Division 182, Creed C. Burlingame, forwarded to the Casualties and Allotments Section seventy-eight letters of condolence for the *Flier* crew's next of kin, along with submarine combat insignia and citations.[2]

Such confusion about the fate of the crew was not uncommon. In other submarine tragedies, relatives sometimes learned of the loss of their loved ones through media reports. For instance, the wife of Earle Caffrey "Penrod" Schneider, commander of the *Dorado*, first heard the news of her husband's death on the radio. At the time, she was driving cross-country with her young son from New London to meet her husband on the West Coast.[3] Alice Allyn Grenkowicz, married to a *Darter* crew member, heard on the radio that his submarine had run aground, but it was a month later when she finally learned that her husband was unharmed; she continued to suffer anxiety attacks for the rest of the war. Many relatives had to rely on individual initiative to find out what had happened to their loved ones. Ann Cottongin, after hearing that the USS *Darter* had been lost at sea with her husband, wrote to her congressman to find out the fate of the crew.[4] Miscommunication and misinformation would remain features of naval disasters throughout the war.

Even at the best of times, communication with family could be difficult. Submariners who wanted to telephone loved ones from Pearl Harbor had to make an advance application, including any names and places likely to be mentioned in the conversation. Eventually regulations banned them from telephoning altogether.[5] Some submariners wrote to their wives or other family members on a daily basis, but their letters could not be mailed—and none received—until they were in port. The American military machine recognized that efficient mail service was a central element of morale, but letters often arrived sporadically and were invariably censored. There was also a degree of self-censorship, in that those writing home often tried to minimize the risks they faced.[6]

Only recently, with the advent of e-mail, have submariners

been able to communicate regularly with their families. Even so, being married to a submariner continues to be emotionally draining, with each prolonged absence capable of eliciting a "grief response."[7] During World War II the wives of submariners typically returned home to live with their parents or tried to find accommodations near a major port. The sense of separation could be especially acute for newlyweds. William Godfrey met his wife while assigned to a newly constructed submarine at Manitowoc, Wisconsin; they married after a whirlwind courtship. Only after arriving at Fremantle did Godfrey learn that he was the father of a daughter—some two months after her birth.[8] Betty Thomson recalled that many of the Americans she met at the Red Cross club in Perth were homesick. One submariner talked incessantly about his family and cried when he received news that his wife had had a baby.[9]

Some couples worked out their own codes for evading censorship. A motor machinist's mate from USS *Dace,* for example, wrote to his wife that "Pa and Ma are doing fine" to let her know that he was in Panama.[10] Some submariners were able to communicate with their families through friends they made in Australia. Norma Black Royle recalled that two sailors from the USS *Swordfish* often visited her home in Perth. Since personal letters were not censored, her mother wrote to the sailors' mothers back in Kentucky to let them know that their sons were safe and well. Royle said that when they received a letter from the sister of one of the submariners, informing them that the *Swordfish* had been lost at sea, "the news shattered us."[11]

The wives of submarine officers constituted another informal network for disseminating news on the fate of loved ones. These women often formed close bonds. So when Slade Cutter's former executive officer, Willis Manning "Tommy" Thomas, was lost with the *Pompano,* Cutter alerted his wife, who was living at Vallejo, California. Cutter's wife, Frannie, was thus prepared to comfort Thomas's widow when the bad news came.[12]

Those higher up in the navy hierarchy or those related to particularly esteemed personnel were often privy to more information. Following the loss of the USS *Harder*, Charles Lockwood wrote personally to Sam Dealey's mother, concluding, "my entire Command extends its deepest sympathy to you, to his wife and children, in your sorrow."[13] Admiral Chester Nimitz wrote to Dealey's uncle, Dallas newspaper editor George Bannerman Dealey. Nimitz's letter emphasized Dealey's excellent patrol record and alluded to the possibility of a Medal of Honor. He also tried to offer a measure of closure: "I cannot honestly encourage you to believe that he escaped the destruction of his ship, for, as you know, survivors from missing submarines are very few."[14]

After hearing the news of the *Robalo*'s loss, Admiral Ernest King personally arranged for Husband Kimmel, still enduring the investigation into his role in the attack on Pearl Harbor, to be flown to New York so that he could be with his wife as they awaited word about their son, Manning. Kimmel's other son, Thomas, was relieved from submarine duty and sent back to a desk job in Washington, D.C. Ralph Christie would later receive some ultra intelligence suggesting that Manning Kimmel had survived, and he discussed the matter with Tom Kimmel, who decided that the information was too indefinite to pass on to his parents.[15]

In a letter dated 14 December 1944, John Crowley wrote to the Casualties Section of the Bureau of Naval Personnel indicating that he had been "deluged" with letters from the crew's relatives wanting to know the particulars of the *Flier*'s loss. He also forwarded to the bureau, for its approval, a draft of a letter that he proposed to send to the relatives; five days later he received a telephone call giving him official clearance to do so. In the letter, Crowley told of the explosion that sank the *Flier* and briefly outlined the fate of those who had managed to swim to land. He held out some hope of other survivors, stating, "It is possible that some members of the crew may have escaped later from undamaged compartments." He concluded: "I feel that it was a miraculous chain of circumstances that permitted any of us to return, and inasmuch as the will of the Almighty is beyond human understanding, I can only join with you in the hope that in some way your prayers for [relative's name]'s safe return may be answered."[16]

The hope held out by Crowley may have tempered the shock and sense of loss experienced by the families. Details about the *Flier*'s loss also lent an air of reality, if not finality, to the deaths of husbands, sons, and brothers, in the absence of bodies and funerals. It was not until January 1946, however, that those who went down with the *Flier* were officially designated "dead" as opposed to "missing in action." In part, this was done on compassionate grounds, since it allowed the wives to continue receiving their husbands' pay, which otherwise would have been terminated.[17]

The Tomb of the Unknown Soldier, created at Arlington National Cemetery after World War I, provided a place of mourning for the families of those who died on the battlefield and whose bodies were never recovered. Many bereaved wives and mothers actually convinced themselves that the interred body was in fact their husband or son.[18] But even this illusion was denied to the relatives of submariners. In the tradition of the sea, victims remained interred in their wrecks, often at unknown locations. The absence of a body or grave site made any sense of closure extremely difficult.[19]

Relatives could cling to the hope that their loved ones might turn up at a hospital or a prison camp. Even fellow submariners were not immune to such fantasies. For instance, after hearing that the USS *Barbel* had gone down with his former Naval Academy roommate and good friend Layton Goodman, Paul Schratz consoled himself that Goodman might have made it to an island.[20] And occasionally, such hopes were realized. Some survivors from the USS *Tang* returned to the United States after being declared killed in action.[21]

With no direct evidence of death, there often came denial. As late as November 1947, Crowley advised the Casualties Section that he was still receiving correspondence from the widow of Lieutenant Paul Knapp. She insisted on knowing the exact location where the *Flier* had gone down. Crowley promised that he would send her a map with the position marked, but the Bureau of Personnel vetoed this as "inadvisable." On 19 November 1947 the bureau wrote to Mrs. Knapp, telling her that although it was "impracticable" to send her a chart, it would provide the estimated coordinates of the submarine's sinking.[22]

Those left to mourn the dead included not only wives, parents, and siblings but also children. Some of the crew on the *Flier* had infants they had never seen or held. One of them—Walter Edward Dorricott Jr. of Philadelphia—had completed his training at the Submarine School in January 1944 and served on the *Flier* as yeoman second class. When officially declared dead in 1946, he left not only a widow, Barbara Maynard Dorricott, but also a seventeen-month-old son he had never laid eyes on.[23]

Epilogue

John Crowley's career survived two formal inquiries, and before the war was over, he was given command of another brand-new submarine. Crowley took charge of the USS *Irex* (SS-482), launched on 26 January 1945 and commissioned on 14 May 1945. The *Irex* was one of twenty-five new Tench class submarines built between 1944 and 1946. These submarines represented a further evolution of the American fleet boat, with a reduced silhouette, better internal layout, and improved machinery. With stronger hulls, the Tench class had a test depth of more than 400 feet. Eventually the *Irex* became the first U.S. submarine fitted with a snorkel, allowing it to use its diesel engines while submerged.

James Liddell continued as Crowley's executive officer on the *Irex*. For the superstitious or the wary (a high proportion of submariners), the two men's history with the *Flier* might be seen as either a bad omen or a lucky charm. Like aviators and bomber crews, those on submarine duty were especially alert to any signs that might alter their odds of survival. Given the *Flier*'s fate, at least one *Irex* crew member requested a transfer, only to have it denied. In any case, the *Irex* would never see combat. The submarine sailed for the Pacific, but the war ended as it was taking on supplies in the Panama Canal Zone. The *Irex* returned to Key West, Florida, to join Submarine Squadron Four.

Even without the threat of Japanese antisubmarine measures,

however, the *Irex* would experience some harrowing moments. During a training dive off Key West, the submarine faced imminent disaster when, already approaching its test depth, seawater began spraying into the maneuvering room. It was later discovered that a three-quarter-inch plug had blown out of the circulating water system. The high-pressure water knocked out the control panel for the lighting and electrical indicators, and the diving planes jammed into a steep dive, taking the *Irex* below its design depth. Fortunately, Crowley immediately recognized the problem and ordered the crew to "blow the negative" and change the planes. The submarine finally nosed toward the surface.[1]

In January 1946 Norvell G. Ward replaced Crowley as skipper of the *Irex*. At the same time, both Crowley and Ward were awarded the Legion of Merit Medal. Ward received the award for his sixth war patrol in command of the USS *Guardfish*. Crowley's award, however, was described by the *New London Day* as "most unusual." The citation referred not to his heroic submarine exploits but to his survival after the loss of the *Flier*.[2] Crowley remained in the navy until 31 March 1961, holding a number of administrative positions, including fleet operations officer and deputy chief of staff to the commander of the Seventh Fleet during the Korean War.[3]

Even for those submariners who left the service at the end of the war, their wartime experiences were never far away. Many remained active in submarine veterans groups, attended reunions, and kept in touch with former crewmates. An enduring spirit of camaraderie served as both a compensation for and a reminder of the dangers faced in war.[4]

Among those who attended reunions of the USS *Redfin* crew was Carlos Placido, one of the American coast watchers who had helped organize the evacuation of the *Flier* survivors. On 29 September 1945 Placido and his fellow coast watchers were awarded Bronze Stars for their efforts. After the war Placido returned to his bakery business in Laguna Beach, California. He retired in 1982 and died of cancer on 10 November 2000 at the age of ninety-four.[5]

After the war the *Redfin*'s skipper, Marshall "Cy" Austin, commanded other submarines, as well as the Submarine School in New London. Like Crowley, he retired from the navy in 1961. He continued working for civilian defense industries and even acted as a consultant for the Hollywood film *Ice Station Zebra*. After surviving two earlier bouts of cancer, Austin died of heart failure on 19 July 2005, at age ninety-four. As it happened, Austin's fellow sub skipper, Norvell G. Ward, also died of heart failure the same day.[6]

John Crowley made little effort to keep in touch with the surviving *Flier* crew after the war, perhaps feeling that it was better to let some memories slip away. The *Flier* survivors only rarely corresponded with one another, and there would be only one reunion, at Annapolis in 1994, fifty years after the *Flier*'s loss.[7]

Earl Baumgart would later work to obtain a posthumous award for James Francis P. Cahl, the shipmate who had drowned after being washed overboard at Midway. Baumgart felt aggrieved that Cahl's family had received only a letter of condolence for his loss. Partly due to Baumgart's efforts, Cahl's name would be included on a waterfront memorial at the USS *Bowfin* Submarine Park honoring submariners lost during World War II.[8]

When the war ended, Alvin Jacobson was at the Panama Canal with the USS *Ling,* on his way back to the Pacific. Discharged from the navy six months later, Jacobson joined his father's brass foundry in Grand Haven, Michigan. He would later become director of the company, with responsibility for hundreds of employees. He married at age thirty-three and fathered two sons and a daughter. He retired at age seventy, and at this writing, he is the only living survivor from the USS *Flier*.[9]

Eventually fishermen in Balabac Strait claimed that they had located the hulk of the *Flier* in waters about 360 feet deep. To date, the wreck remains unexplored. An underwater survey might be able to confirm whether the *Flier* hit a mine and determine the extent of the damage caused. The question that remained uppermost in Jacobson's mind, however, was whether the escape hatches over the forward and aft torpedo rooms were open. Had men remained alive in the sunken submarine?

In May 1998, fifty-four years after the most harrowing events of his life, Jacobson made a pilgrimage to the spot where the *Flier* went down. Accompanied by his son Steve, he retraced the route the survivors had taken to Brooke's Point. They also visited Puerto Princesa and the site of the Japanese massacre of POWs. On Bugsuk Island they found the water cistern the survivors had drunk from more than half a century earlier. Most things had changed, however. The once sparsely populated area of Brooke's Point had become a town of 40,000 people. What had not changed was the emotion that welled up as Jacobson stood on the bow of a ship sailing over the site of the USS *Flier*'s final resting place.

Notes

Abbreviations

CBC   Clay Blair Collection, American Heritage Center, University of Wyoming, Laramie

JAG   Judge Advocate General, Department of the Navy, Washington, D.C.

NARA   National Archives and Records Administration, College Park, Maryland

SFM   Submarine Force Museum, Groton, Connecticut

UBSM   USS *Bowfin* Submarine Museum, Pearl Harbor, Hawaii

Prologue

1. T. O. Paine, *The Transpacific Voyage of His Imperial Japanese Majesty's Submarine I-400 (Tom Paine's Journal, July–Dec. 1945)* (self-published, 1984), 7–8.

2. Ernest J. King and Walter Muir Whitehill, *Fleet Admiral King: A Naval Record* (London: Eyre and Spottiswoode, 1953), 392–93.

1. The Aleutians

1. Thomas Parrish, *The Submarine: A History* (London: Viking Penguin, 2004), 337. See also David Jones and Peter Nunan, *U.S. Subs Down Under: Brisbane, 1942–1945* (Annapolis, Md.: Naval Institute Press, 2005), 27; Dan Van Der Vat, *Stealth at Sea: The History of the Submarine* (London: Orion, 1995), 170; Stuart S. Murray, *The Reminiscences of Admiral Stuart S. Murray* (1974; reprint, Annapolis, Md.: U.S. Naval Institute, 2001), 86.

2. J. D. Crowley file, UBSM.

3. Biographical files on Captain John D. Crowley, Naval Historical Center, Washington Navy Yard, Washington, D.C.; Skippers of U.S. World War II Pacific Ocean Submarine Patrols—John Daniel Crowley,

box 67, folder 2, CBC; John D. Crowley Military Personnel Records, National Personnel Records Center, St. Louis, Mo.

4. W. J. Holmes, *Undersea Victory: The Influence of Submarine Operations on the War in the Pacific* (New York: Doubleday, 1966), 34.

5. Stephen Budiansky, *Battle of Wits: The Complete Story of Codebreaking in World War II* (London: Viking, 2000), 3; Edwin T. Layton, *"And I Was There": Pearl Harbor and Midway—Breaking the Secrets* (1985; reprint, Annapolis, Md.: Naval Institute Press, 2006), 385.

6. Foster Hailey, *Pacific Battle Line* (New York: Macmillan, 1944), 331.

7. John Crowley, narrative recorded at Pearl Harbor, 2 October 1944, box 67, folder 2, CBC (hereafter, Crowley narrative); USS *S-28* First War Patrol Report, 20 May, 2 June, 18 June 1942, UBSM.

8. Crowley narrative; Harry Holmes, *The Last Patrol* (Annapolis, Md.: Naval Institute Press, 1994), 25.

9. USS *S-28* First War Patrol Report, Health and Habitability.

10. See Fleet Type Submarine Online, http://www.maritime.org/fleetsub/index.htm (accessed 13 December 2005).

11. USS *S-28* Second War Patrol Report, UBSM. See also USS *Wahoo* Fourth War Patrol Report, Major Defects, in *U.S.S. Wahoo (SS-238) American Submarine War Patrol Reports,* ed. J. T. McDaniel (Riverdale, Ga.: Riverdale Books, 2003), 86.

12. USS *S-28* Third War Patrol Report, UBSM.

13. Quoted in Jones and Nunan, *Subs Down Under,* 49.

14. Bobette Gugliotta, *Pigboat 39: An American Sub Goes to War* (Lexington: University Press of Kentucky, 1984), 139–40, 196–212; Murray, *Reminiscences,* 149.

15. Walter Karig and Eric Purdon, *Battle Report: Pacific War, Middle Phase* (New York: Rinehart, 1947), 263; USS *S-28* First War Patrol Report, Remarks.

16. Holmes, *The Last Patrol,* 23; Paine, *Transpacific Voyage,* 19.

17. Crowley narrative; Jones and Nunan, *Subs Down Under,* 74, 125.

18. Ralph Waldo Christie, taped interview, box 97, folders 2–5, CBC; John D. Alden, *The Fleet Submarine in the U.S. Navy: A Design and Construction History* (London: Arms and Armour Press, 1979), 83.

19. USS *S-28* Fourth War Patrol Report, endorsement, UBSM.

20. USS *S-28* Fifth War Patrol Report, endorsement; Health and Habitability, UBSM; Karig and Purdon, *Battle Report: Pacific War,* 264.

21. John D. Crowley to Aldona Sendzikas, 30 March 1992, J. D. Crowley File, UBSM.

22. Quoted in Karig and Purdon, *Battle Report: Pacific War,* 264.

23. James F. DeRose, *Unrestricted Warfare: How a New Breed of Officers Led the Submarine Force to Victory in World War II* (New York:

John Wiley and Sons, 2000), 112; Hailey, *Pacific Battle Line*, 368; Karig and Purdon, *Battle Report: Pacific War*, 334.

24. Quoted in Karig and Purdon, *Battle Report: Pacific War*, 343. See also Thomas B. Buell, *Master of Sea Power: A Biography of Fleet Admiral Ernest J. King* (Boston: Little, Brown, 1980), 355–56, 398; Galen Roger Perras, *Stepping Stones to Nowhere: The Aleutian Islands, Alaska, and American Military Strategy, 1867–1945* (Vancouver, B.C.: UBC Press, 2003), 127, 133, 150, 155; James W. Hamilton and William J. Bolce Jr., *Gateway to Victory: The Wartime Story of the San Francisco Army Port of Embarkation* (Stanford, Calif.: Stanford University Press, 1946), 101–2.

25. Holmes, *The Last Patrol*, 113; A. J. Hill, *Under Pressure: The Final Voyage of Submarine S-Five* (New York: New American Library, 2002), 206; Holmes, *Undersea Victory*, 356; Commander Submarine Force, U.S. Pacific Fleet, http://www.csp.navy.mil/ww2boats/ (accessed 23 August 2004).

2. A New Boat

1. Crowley narrative; biographical file on Captain John D. Crowley, Naval Historical Center; Paul R. Schratz, *Submarine Commander: A Story of World War II and Korea* (Lexington: University Press of Kentucky, 1988), 29–30, 39, 41, 83.

2. Press release, "Launching of Submarine 'Flier,'" 8 July 1943, USS *Flier* Scrapbook, SFM; Van Der Vat, *Stealth at Sea*, 35; Buell, *Master of Sea Power*, 58; Ken Henry and Don Keith, *Gallant Lady: A Biography of the USS* Archerfish (New York: Tom Doherty Associates, 2004), 57; Alden, *Fleet Submarine*, 78; Philip Kaplan, *Run Silent* (Annapolis, Md.: Naval Institute Press, 2002), 42–43.

3. Slade D. Cutter, *The Reminiscences of Captain Slade D. Cutter* (Annapolis, Md.: U.S. Naval Institute, 1985), 257, 303.

4. I. I. Yates, Supervisor of Shipbuilding, to Electric Boat Company, 22 June 1943; Alfred Lawton, Secretary to Senator Smith, to L. Y. Spear, President of Electric Boat Company, 29 June 1943, *Flier* Scrapbook, SFM; Marine Engineering and Shipping Review (no date); press release, "Winners for Cutting Lost Time," 12 July 1943, *Flier* Scrapbook, SFM; Biographical Directory of the United States Congress, http://www.geocities.com/Colosseum/Track/3059/Rufinopart3.html?20069 (accessed 2 November 2005).

5. Schratz, *Submarine Commander*, 88–89. See also Cutter, *Reminiscences*, 350; memorandum for Mr. Robinson, 30 June 1943, *Flier* Scrapbook, SFM.

6. A. D. Barnes to G. R. Donaho, 12 July 1943, *Flier* Scrapbook, SFM.

7. USS *Flier*—SS 250 Launch Program, *Flier* Scrapbook, SFM.

8. U.S. Navy Bureau of Ships, *Submarine Material Guide* (Washington, D.C.: U.S. Navy, 1944), 1–2, 14.

9. See C. Kenneth Ruiz with John Bruning, *The Luck of the Draw: The Memoir of a World War II Submariner* (St. Paul, Minn.: Zenith Press, 2005), 96; Mark P. Parillo, *The Japanese Merchant Marine in World War II* (Annapolis, Md.: Naval Institute Press, 1993), 159.

10. Charles Andrews, taped interview, box 96, folder 15, CBC; Van Der Vat, *Stealth at Sea,* 170; Crowley narrative; Hill, *Under Pressure,* 52; Holmes, *Undersea Victory,* 40; Gary E. Weir and Walter J. Boyne, *Rising Tide: The Untold Story of the Russian Submarines that Fought the Cold War* (New York: Basic Books, 2003), 21.

11. Calvin Moon and William Godfrey Jr. interviews, Rutgers Oral History Archives of World War II, http://fashistory.rutgers.edu/oralhistory/orlhom.htm (accessed 2 September 2005); Alden, *Fleet Submarine,* 85; Schratz, *Submarine Commander,* 24–25; Ruiz, *Luck of the Draw,* 105.

12. James Liddell narrative, 2 October 1944, box 67, folder 2, CBC (hereafter, Liddell narrative); Bart Bartholomew, "Submarine School," *Polaris,* April 1994, http://www.subvetpaul.com/SAGA_4_94.htm (accessed 1 July 2005); George Wells and William Godfrey Jr. interviews, Rutgers Oral History Archives.

13. Liddell narrative; Clay Blair Jr., *Silent Victory: The U.S. Submarine War against Japan* (1975; reprint, Annapolis, Md.: Naval Institute Press, 2001), 592.

14. Earl Baumgart, *Badger State Newsletter,* January–February 1996, *Flier* File, UBSM.

3. Midway

1. Robert J. Cressman et al., *"A Glorious Page in Our History": The Battle of Midway, 4–6 June 1942* (Missoula, Mont.: Pictorial Histories, 1990), 1–2, 4, 7, 11; Gregory F. Michno, USS Pampanito: *Killer-Angel* (Norman: University of Oklahoma Press, 2000), 161; Midway Islands, The World Factbook, http://www.cia.gov/ciia/publications/factbook/geos/mq.html (accessed 17 September 2004); Midway Islands History, http://www.janeresture.com.midway/ (accessed 17 September 2004).

2. Budiansky, *Battle of Wits,* 15; Mark Healy, *Midway 1942: Turning Point in the Pacific* (1993; reprint, Oxford: Osprey, 2004), 13; Layton, *"And I Was There,"* 407; Stephen Howarth, *To Shining Sea: A History of the United States Navy, 1774–1991* (New York: Random House, 1991), 404–5.

3. Philip Warner, *Secret Forces of World War II* (1985; reprint, Barnsley, U.K.: Pen and Sword, 2004), 140; Jeffrey M. Moore, *Spies for Nimitz: Joint Military Intelligence in the Pacific War* (Annapolis, Md.: Naval Institute Press, 2004), 7; Karig and Purdon, *Battle Report: Pacific War,* 33.

4. E. B. Potter and Chester W. Nimitz, eds., *The Great Sea War: The Story of Naval Action in World War II* (Englewood Cliffs, N.J.: Prentice-Hall, 1960), 224–25, 234, 241; Larry Kimmett and Margaret Regis, *U.S. Submarines in World War II: An Illustrated History* (Seattle: Navigator Publishing, 1996), 44–45; Hugh Bicheno, *Midway* (London: Cassell, 2001), 64; Steven Trent Smith, *The Rescue: A True Story of Courage and Survival in World War II* (New York: John Wiley and Sons, 2001), 71, 259; Holmes, *Undersea Victory,* 134; Cressman, *"A Glorious Page,"* 19; Healy, *Midway 1942,* 88; Layton, *"And I Was There,"* 447; Craig Burke, "The Principle of the Objective: Nagumo vs Spruance at Midway," http://www.centruyinter.net/midway/objective.html (accessed 27 July 2005).

5. Quoted in King and Whitehill, *Fleet Admiral King,* 171. See also Reminiscences of Admiral James Fife, Oral History Memoir transcript, 1962, 296–97, Columbia University, New York; Ronald H. Spector, *At War at Sea: Sailors and Naval Combat in the Twentieth Century* (New York: Viking, 2001), 202; Joan Beaumont, ed., *Australia's War: 1939–45* (Sydney: Allen and Unwin, 1996), 36; Healy, *Midway 1942,* 89; Warner, *Secret Forces,* 140–41.

6. Murray, *Reminiscences,* 215–16; Van Der Vat, *Stealth at Sea,* 296.

7. Bill Gleason, "Diary of a War Patrol—USS *Gurnard* (SS 254)," *Polaris,* June 1985, http://www.subvetpaul.com/SAGA_6_85.htm (accessed 1 July 2005).

8. Ruiz, *Luck of the Draw,* 181.

9. Godfrey interview; Cutter, *Reminiscences,* 252; Schratz, *Submarine Commander,* 75–76; Fife reminiscences, 188; Forest J. Sterling, *Wake of the Wahoo* (Philadelphia: Chilton, 1960), 156–57.

10. Cressman, *"A Glorious Page,"* 2, 9; Final Investigative Report into the Grounding of the USS *Flier* (SS-250) on January 16, 1944, JAG, Record of Proceedings, 1 February 1944, 2; I. J. Galantin, *Take Her Deep! A Submarine against Japan in World War II* (Chapel Hill, N.C.: Algonquin Books, 1987), 156–57; Midway Islands History; Midway Islands, The World Factbook.

11. Final Investigative Report into the Grounding of the USS *Flier,* Finding of Facts, Record of Proceedings, 1 February 1944, 3.

12. Earl Baumgart, 21 December 1991, *Flier* File, UBSM.

4. Grounded

1. Examination of John Crowley, 1 February 1944, Final Investigative Report into the Grounding of the USS *Flier,* Record of Proceedings, 3.

2. Earl Baumgart to Admiral I. J. Galantin, 10 November 1992, *Flier* File, UBSM.

3. Examination of James Liddell, 3 February 1944, Record of Proceedings, 36.

4. Examination of Herbert A. Baehr, 3 February 1944, Record of Proceedings, 38.

5. Examination of Waite H. Daggy, 3 February 1944, Record of Proceedings, 43; Baumgart to Galantin, 10 November 1992; Earl Baumgart, 21 December 1991, *Flier* File, UBSM.

6. Examination of Kenneth Leroy Gwinn, 3 February 1944, Record of Proceedings, 39–40.

7. Examination of Joseph A. Lia, 3 February 1944, Record of Proceedings, 42.

5. USS *Macaw*

1. Extracts from *Flier*'s Signal Book, Exhibits, Final Investigative Report into the Grounding of the USS *Flier,* JAG.

2. USS *Macaw,* http://www.hawaiireef.noaa.gov/research/MA/macaw.html (accessed 14 September 2004); NavSource Online, http://www.navsource.org/ (accessed 14 September 2004); Peter Maas, *The Terrible Hours: The Man behind the Greatest Submarine Rescue in History* (New York: Harper Torch, 1999), 163–64, 187.

3. Maas, *Terrible Hours,* 32, 61–62, 119, 143, 152.

4. Galantin, *Take Her Deep,* 157; Bartholomew, "Submarine School"; Parrish, *The Submarine,* 405.

5. Examination of John Crowley, 1 February 1944, Record of Proceedings, 7–10.

6. Earl Baumgart, 21 December 1991, *Flier* File, UBSM.

7. William P. Mack and Royal W. Connell, *Naval Ceremonies, Customs and Traditions* (Annapolis, Md.: Naval Institute Press, 1980), 177, 180; Burial at Sea, http://www.hsitory.navy.mil/faqs/faq85–1.htm (accessed 20 October 2004).

8. Baumgart, 21 December 1991, *Flier* File, UBSM.

9. Ruiz, *Luck of the Draw,* 271. See also Christopher McKee, *Sober Men and True: Sailor Lives in the Royal Navy, 1900–1945* (Cambridge, Mass.: Harvard University Press, 2002), 125; Joy Damousi, *The Labour*

of Loss: Mourning, Memory and Wartime Bereavement in Australia (Cambridge: Cambridge University Press, 1999), 119.

10. Henry and Keith, *Gallant Lady*, 45–46.

11. Examination of Crowley, 1 February 1944, Record of Proceedings, 8.

12. Galantin, *Take Her Deep*, 156–57.

13. William Tuohy, *The Bravest Man: The Story of Richard O'Kane and U.S. Submariners in the Pacific War* (Thrupp Stroud, U.K.: Sutton, 2002), 212; DeRose, *Unrestricted Warfare*, 202; Wreck Sites Midway Atoll, http://www.hawaiianatolls.org/research/NOWRAMP2002/journals/midwaywrecks.php (accessed 17 March 2006).

6. Board of Investigation

1. Examination of John Crowley, 1 February 1944, Record of Proceedings, 9.

2. Blair, *Silent Victory*, 432, 592–93.

3. C. A. Lockwood to John B. Longstaff, 25 January 1944, JAG; Blair, *Silent Victory*, 431–32.

4. USS *Bushnell* AS-15 (submarine tender), http://www.atule.com/uss_bushnell.htm (accessed 15 March 2006); Tender Tale, United States Navy, Submarine Tenders, USS *Bushnell* AS 15, http://www.mississippi.net/~comcents/tendertale.com/tenders/115/115.html (accessed 15 March 2006).

5. See Holmes, *Undersea Victory*, 34; Hill, *Under Pressure*, 114, 199; Fife reminiscences, 427; Moon interview, 13.

6. Schratz, *Submarine Commander*, 78–79; Tuohy, *The Bravest Man*, 212; Blair, *Silent Victory*, 460.

7. Final Investigative Report into the Grounding of the USS *Flier*, Finding of Facts, 71.

8. Examination of John Crowley, 1 February 1944, Record of Proceedings, 11.

9. Examination of Benjamin E. Adams Jr., 2 February 1944, Record of Proceedings, 24.

10. Examination of Crowley, 5 February 1944, Record of Proceedings, 64–65.

11. Final Investigative Report, Opinion, 72–73.

12. Endorsement of C. A. Lockwood to Final Investigative Report, JAG.

13. Baumgart, *Badger State Newsletter*, January–February 1996.

14. Examination of James Liddell, 3 February 1944, Record of Proceedings, 34.

15. Examination of Kenneth Leroy Gwinn, 3 February 1944, Record of Proceedings, 40. See also examination of Herbert A. Baehr and George J. Banchero, ibid., 38, 45.

16. Examination of Joseph A. Lia and Waite H. Daggy, 3 February 1944, Record of Proceedings, 42–44.

17. See, for example, Mike Ostlund, *Find 'Em, Chase 'Em, Sink 'Em: The Mysterious Loss of the WWII Submarine USS* Gudgeon (Guilford, Conn.: Lyons Press, 2006), 144, 151; Ruiz, *Luck of the Draw,* 91; James H. Patric, *To War in a Tin Can: A Memoir of World War II aboard a Destroyer* (Jefferson, N.C.: McFarland, 2004), 26.

18. Navy Department, Office of the Judge Advocate General, 1 September 1944, JAG.

7. Resumed Patrol

1. Crowley narrative, 22; Final Investigative Report into the Grounding of the USS *Flier,* JAG.

2. See Doug Stanton, *In Harm's Way* (New York: St. Martin's Paperbacks, 2002), 16–19; Bruce M. Petty, *At War in the Pacific: Personal Accounts of World War II Navy and Marine Corps Officers* (Jefferson, N.C.: McFarland, 2006), 187–89.

3. Wells interview.

4. Moon interview. See also Hamilton and Bolce, *Gateway to Victory,* 152.

5. Galantin, *Take Her Deep,* 193, 195.

6. Blair, *Silent Victory,* 592.

7. Benjamin Ernest Adams Jr. File, UBSM; Baumgart, *Badger State Newsletter,* January–February 1996.

8. Alvin E. Jacobson to author, 12 May 2006.

9. Liddell narrative, 10, 12.

10. USS *Flier* First War Patrol Report, 4 June 1944, UBSM. See also Norman Friedman, *Submarine Design and Development* (London: Conway Maritime, 1984), 52.

11. Alvin Jacobson, *Survivor's Story: Submarine USS* Flier (self-published, 1997; revised, 2002), 61.

12. Howarth, *To Shining Sea,* 435–36; Ostlund, *Find 'Em,* 168; Henry and Keith, *Gallant Lady,* 38.

13. Quoted in Spector, *At War at Sea,* 243.

14. Crowley narrative, 23; USS *Flier* First War Patrol Report, 5 June 1944; John D. Alden, *U.S. Submarine Attacks during World War II* (Annapolis, Md.: Naval Institute Press, 1989), 104; Healey, *Mid-*

way 1942, 24; United States Strategic Bombing Survey (Pacific), Interrogation of Japanese Officials, Aleutian Campaign, http://www.ibiblio .org/hyperwar/AAF/USSBS/IJO/IJO-24.html (accessed 10 November 2005).

15. Crowley narrative, 24.

16. Alden, *U.S. Submarine Attacks,* 106; CV-14 *Ticonderoga,* http:// pacific.valka.cz/ships/usn/cv/cv-14.htm (accessed 10 November 2005).

17. USS *Flier* First War Patrol Report, 13 June 1944.

18. Jacobson, *Survivor's Story,* 63. See also Schratz, *Submarine Commander,* 71–72.

19. Liddell narrative, 14.

20. Jacobson, *Survivor's Story,* 63–64; Holmes, *Undersea Victory,* 299, 334.

21. Moore, *Spies for Nimitz,* 99; Frank Gibney, ed., *Senso: The Japanese Remember the Pacific War,* trans. Beth Cary (London: M.E. Sharpe, 1995), 127; King and Whitehill, *Fleet Admiral King,* 350; John W. Dower, *War without Mercy: Race and Power in the Pacific War* (New York: Pantheon Books, 1986), 246.

22. Crowley narrative, 25.

23. Jacobson, *Survivor's Story,* 65.

24. Liddell narrative, 13; USS *Flier* First War Patrol Report, 22, 23 June 1944.

25. Alden, *U.S. Submarine Attacks,* 108.

26. Jacobson, *Survivor's Story,* 67.

27. Liddell narrative, 9; USS *Flier* (SS-250), http://ussubvetsofworldwarii. org/ss_submarines/ss250.htm (accessed 19 August 2004); *Flier* (SS-250), http://www.subvetpaul.com/LostBoats/Flier.htm (accessed 9 August 2004).

28. USS *Flier* First War Patrol Report, endorsement by R. W. Christie, 18 July 1944; endorsement by H. H. McLean, 10 July 1944.

29. Quoted in Buell, *Master of Sea Power,* 381. See also Department of the Navy—Naval Historical Center, http://www.history.navy.mil (accessed 23 August 2004).

30. Blair, *Silent Victory,* 640–41; Keith M. Milton, *Subs against the Rising Sun* (Las Cruces, N.M.: Yucca Tree Press, 2000), 127.

31. See Holmes, *Undersea Victory,* 260; Alden, *U.S. Submarine Attacks,* ix; Potter and Nimitz, *Great Sea War,* 408–9.

8. Fremantle

1. Jacobson, *Survivor's Story,* 68.

2. Lewis Sebring quoted in *West Australian,* 1 August 1944, 4.

3. *West Australian,* 5 July 1944, 2.

4. Quoted in John Edwards, *Curtin's Gift: Reinterpreting Australia's Greatest Prime Minister* (Sydney: Allen and Unwin, 2005), 2.

5. Quoted in David Walker, "Shooting Mabel: Warrior Masculinity and Asian Invasion," *History Australia* 2, no. 3 (December 2005): 89.

6. Norma Black Royle interview, 29 November 2005.

7. Jacqui Sherriff, "Fremantle South Slipway: A Vital World War II Defence Facility," *Fremantle Studies* 2, no. 2 (2002): 106, 109–10; John Dowson, *Old Fremantle: Photographs, 1850–1950* (Perth: University of Western Australia Press, 2003), 214; Tom Frame, *Pacific Partners: A History of Australian-American Naval Relations* (Sydney: Hodder and Stroughton, 1992), 75.

8. Gleason, "Diary of a War Patrol—USS *Gurnard* (SS 245)."

9. Godfrey interview.

10. Quoted in Bart Bartholomew, The Fremantle Submarine Base, http://www.subvetpaul.com/TheFremantle.htm (accessed 30 July 2004).

11. Quoted in *A Small War: Corvettes—The 39 through Fremantle* (Perth: West Australian Newspapers, 1991), 7.

12. *Fremantle Gazette,* 3 October 1984, 6.

13. Sterling, *Wake of the Wahoo,* 123, 200. See also Gugilotta, *Pigboat 39,* 179; David E. Stannard, *Honor Killing: How the Infamous "Massie Affair" Transformed Hawai'i* (New York: Viking, 2005), 416; Don Keith, *In the Course of Duty: The Heroic Mission of the USS* Batfish (New York: NAL Caliber, 2005), 137–38.

14. Elizabeth Thomson interview, 30 September 2006.

15. Adrian Wood, ed., *If This Should Be Farewell: A Family Separated by War* (Fremantle, Australia: Fremantle Arts Centre Press, 2003), 41.

16. *Sunday Times,* 23 July 1944, 2; Kate Darian-Smith, "War and Australian Society," in Beaumont, *Australia's War,* 70.

17. *Mirror,* 8 July 1944, 5; ibid., 15 July 1944.

18. Henry and Keith, *Gallant Lady,* 278.

19. Michael Sturma, *Death at a Distance: The Loss of the Legendary USS* Harder (Annapolis, Md.: Naval Institute Press, 2006), 137–43.

20. Christie interview.

21. Schratz, *Submarine Commander,* 43.

22. Christie interview; Ralph Christie to Commander E. E. Yeomans, 5 October 1943, box 65, folder 6, CBC.

23. Andrews interview; John G. Mansfield Jr., *Cruisers for Breakfast: War Patrols of the U.S.S. Darter and U.S.S. Dace* (Tacoma, Wash.: Media Center Publishing, 1997), 228.

24. Ralph Christie to Charles Lockwood, 23 June 1943, box 65, folder 6, CBC.

25. Charles Lockwood to Ralph Christie, 3 July 1943, ibid.

26. Charles Lockwood to Ralph Christie, 20 August 1943, ibid.

27. *Sunday Times,* 9 July 1944, 13.

28. Alvin Jacobson interview, 19 May 2006.

29. Godfrey interview.

30. Jacobson interview.

31. Baumgart, *Badger State Newsletter,* January–February 1996.

9. Death in Thirty Seconds

1. Philip Nichols interview, box 99, folder 13, CBC.

2. R. W. Christie to C. A. Lockwood, 23 June 1943, box 65, folder 6, CBC; Frame, *Pacific Partners,* 75.

3. Alvin E. Jacobson, typescript (no date), 1, *Flier* Scrapbook, SFM.

4. Crowley narrative.

5. See Joseph F. Enright with James W. Ryan, *Shinano! The Sinking of Japan's Secret Supership* (London: Bodley Head, 1987), 73.

6. Parillo, *Japanese Merchant Marine,* 90; Buell, *Master of Sea Power,* 412.

7. Eugene D. McGee, "To Sink and Swim: The USS *Flier,*" *Submarine Review,* October 1996, 95; Blair, *Silent Victory,* 714; Christie interview; Jacobson typescript, 2.

8. Godfrey interview.

9. Chronological Narrative of Second War Patrol of USS *Flier* in Philippines Area, Survival Report, Records of the Office of the Chief of Naval Operations, Record Group 38, NARA (hereafter, Survival Report); Crowley narrative; *New York Times,* 3 December 1944, 31; John D. Crowley (as reported to Bill Wolfe), "Loss of USS *Flier,*" *Polaris,* June 1981, http://www.subvetpaul.com/SAGA_6_81.htm (accessed 1 July 2005).

10. Liddell narrative.

11. Baumgart, *Badger State Newsletter,* January–February 1996.

12. Jacobson typescript, 2–3; Jacobson interview with author, 19 May 2006; Jacobson, *Survivor's Story,* 11. Although some sources indicate that William Reynolds was later sighted in the water, this is contradicted by the records of the Casualty Assistance Branch, Bureau of Naval Personnel, Record Group 38, NARA.

13. Holmes, *The Last Patrol,* 49–50.

14. Edwin Gray, *Few Survived: A Comprehensive Survey of Submarine Accidents and Disasters* (London: Leo Cooper, 1986), 181–83, 188–90; Holmes, *The Last Patrol,* 15, 139.

15. Quoted in *New York Times,* 3 December 1944, 31.

16. See Maas, *Terrible Hours,* 49.

17. Gray, *Few Survived*, 120–21; Hill, *Under Pressure*, 206–7; Parrish, *The Submarine*, 188; Maas, *Terrible Hours*, 71–72.

18. Buell, *Master of Sea Power*, 77.

19. A detailed account of the rescue is given by Maas, *Terrible Hours*. See also Weir and Boyne, *Rising Tide*, 218; Henry and Keith, *Gallant Lady*, 103, 154–57.

20. Van Der Vat, *Stealth at Sea*, 307; Maas, *Terrible Hours*, 292–93, 297, 299.

21. Godfrey interview.

22. Cutter, *Reminiscences*, 161.

23. Quoted in Kaplan, *Run Silent*, 46.

24. Moon interview.

25. DeRose, *Unrestricted Warfare*, 213, 219–20, 224; Cindy Adams, "USS *Tang* Survivors," *Polaris*, February 1981, http://www.subvetpaul .com/SAGA_2_81.htm (accessed 1 July 2005).

26. Alden, *Fleet Submarine*, 18; Fleet Type Submarine Online, 82.

27. Parrish, *The Submarine*, 181; Gray, *Few Survived*, 191–92; Hill, *Under Pressure*, 92, 138.

10. Cause and Effect

1. Crowley, Survival Report.

2. Jacobson typescript, 2.

3. Baumgart, *Badger State Newsletter*, January–February 1996.

4. See, for example, Edwin Hoyt, Bowfin: *The Story of One of America's Fabled Submarines in World War II* (New York: Van Nostrand Reinhold, 1983), 45; Mansfield, *Cruisers for Breakfast*, 152, 201.

5. Christie interview. See also Holmes, *Undersea Victory*, 322, 382; Jones and Nunan, *U.S. Subs Down Under*, 228; Spector, *At War at Sea*, 294; Samuel Eliot Morison, *History of United States Naval Operations in World War II*, vol. 12 (London: Oxford University Press, 1958), 169–74; Potter and Nimitz, *Great Sea War*, 374–75.

6. Crowley, Survival Report.

7. Holmes, *Undersea Victory*, 30–33; Hoyt, Bowfin, 8; Hill, *Under Pressure*, 104; Schratz, *Submarine Commander*, 24, 26; Gugliotta, *Pigboat 39*, 157; Godfrey interview; Maas, *Terrible Hours*, 13, 44.

8. Kimmett and Regis, *U.S. Submarines in World War II*, 85; Michael Gunton, *Dive! Dive! Dive! Submarines at War* (London: Constable, 2003), 240.

9. Sherry Sontag and Christopher Drew, *Blind Man's Bluff: The Untold Story of American Submarine Espionage* (New York: Public Affairs, 1998), 5, 7, 12, 23–24.

10. Weir and Boyne, *Rising Tide,* 79.

11. Sontag and Drew, *Blind Man's Bluff,* 15, 24.

12. Jacobson interview; Jacobson to author, 12 May 2006.

13. Lockwood to Christie, 25 July 1944, box 65, folder 6, CBC.

14. Norman Polmar and Dorr B. Carpenter, *Submarines of the Imperial Japanese Navy, 1904–1945* (London: Conway Maritime Press, 1986), 19, 24, 89; Carl Boyd and Akihiko Yoshida, *The Japanese Submarine Force and World War II* (Shrewsbury, U.K.: Airlife, 1995), 72, 74; Arnold S. Lott, *Most Dangerous Sea: A History of Mine Warfare and an Account of U.S. Navy Mine Warfare Operations in World War II and Korea* (Annapolis, Md.: U.S. Naval Institute Press, 1959), 32, 40; Bob Hackett and Sander Kingsepp, Sensuikan! HIJMS Submarine I-123 and I-124, http://www.combinedfleet.com/I-123.htm (accessed 30 August 2005); WW2 in the Pacific: Countdown to War, http://www.ww2pacific.com/countdown2.htm (accessed 21 September 2004). Sources are contradictory as to whether *I-123* or *I-124* planted mines in Balabac Strait.

15. McGee, "To Sink and Swim," 97–98; Vernon J. Miller to Jack Crowley, 3 September 1985, *Flier* Scrapbook, SFM; Holmes, *Undersea Victory,* 408; Lott, *Most Dangerous Sea,* 58.

16. David Bushnell, http://beatl.barnard.columbia.edu/beatldb/maritimedb/display/persion (accessed 3 May 2006).

17. Lockwood to Christie, 3 July 1943, box 65, folder 6, CBC. See also Christie interview; Gunton, *Dive,* 151–52; Parrish, *The Submarine,* 382; Jones and Nunan, *U.S. Subs Down Under,* 102–3; Kimmett and Regis, *U.S. Submarines in World War II,* 54; Hoyt, *Bowfin,* 82; Holmes, *Undersea Victory,* 225; Van Der Vat, *Stealth at Sea,* 20; Alden, *Fleet Submarine,* 101; Schratz, *Submarine Commander,* 57; Friedman, *Submarine Design,* 32; Jim Christley, *US Submarines, 1941–1945* (New York: Osprey, 2006), 5; Naval Mine History, http://members.aol.com/helmineron/minehist.htm (accessed 21 September 2004).

18. Kimmett and Regis, *U.S. Submarines in World War II,* 54; Holmes, *Undersea Victory,* 225; Lott, *Most Dangerous Sea,* 8, 80, 82; Parillo, *Japanese Merchant Marine,* 195, 201; Military Analysis Network, http://www.fas.org/man/dod-101/sys/ships/weaps/mines.htm (accessed 21 September 2004).

19. Lott, *Most Dangerous Sea,* 67–69; Cutter, *Reminiscences,* 193; Kaplan, *Run Silent,* 121.

20. Schratz, *Submarine Commander,* 149–50, 165; Mansfield, *Cruisers for Breakfast,* 127, 228; Lott, *Most Dangerous Sea,* 264; Kaplan, *Run Silent,* 106.

21. The official U.S. Navy estimate is that three to eight submarines

were sunk by enemy mines; the causes of five other submarine losses are designated "unknown." McDaniel, *U.S.S. Wahoo*, viii.

22. Holmes, *The Last Patrol*, 146; Holmes, *Undersea Victory*, 408; Schratz, *Submarine Commander*, 86; Sontag and Drew, *Blind Man's Bluff*, 88.

23. Smith, *The Rescue*, 291; Christie interview; USS *Crevalle* (SS 291), http://www.cyburban.com/-protrn/crevalle.htm (accessed 1 October 2004).

24. Edward Dissette and H. C. Adamson, *Guerrilla Submarines* (New York: Ballantine, 1972), 157–58.

25. Holmes, *The Last Patrol*, 114–15.

26. USS *Flier* First War Patrol Report, 30 June 1944.

27. Statement of Charles B. McAfoos, Office of Naval Records and History, USS *Robalo* File, UBSM; Charles A. Willoughby, *The Guerrilla Resistance Movement in the Philippines: 1941–1945* (New York: Vantage Press, 1972), 159; Holmes, *Undersea Victory*, 356.

28. Ralph Christie to T. C. Kinkaid, 29 August 1944, box 65, folder 6, CBC.

11. Black Water

1. See R. A. McCance et al., *Hazards to Men in Ships Lost at Sea, 1940–1944* (London: His Majesty's Stationery Office, 1956), 32; Stanton, *In Harm's Way*, 110, 152.

2. Jacobson typescript, 3.

3. Liddell narrative; Crowley, Survival Report; Crowley, "Loss of USS *Flier*."

4. Quoted in *New York Times*, 3 December 1944, 31.

5. Liddell narrative; also quoted in Blair, *Silent Victory*, 715.

6. Penny Lee Dean, *Open Water Swimming* (Champaign, Ill.: Human Kinetics, 1998), 14; McCance, *Hazards to Men in Ships*, 9.

7. Arthur Gibson Howell, statement in Survival Report; *New York Times*, 3 December 1944, 31; USS *Flier* First War Patrol Report, Radar.

8. Liddell narrative.

9. Baumgart, *Badger State Newsletter*, January–February 1996.

10. Mansfield, *Cruisers for Breakfast*, 92–93.

11. Jacobson typescript, 5.

12. Christie interview; Cutter, *Reminiscences*, 587; Ruiz, *Luck of the Draw*, 73.

13. Macdonald Critchley, *Shipwreck-Survivors: A Medical Study* (London: J. and A. Churchill, 1943), 68. See also Stanton, *In Harm's Way*, 167.

14. Jacobson typescript, 5–7.

15. Liddell narrative.

16. Howell statement, Survival Report.

17. Baumgart, *Badger State Newsletter,* January–February 1996.

18. Although contemporary reports agreed that the *Flier* survivors made landfall on Mantangule Island, some of the men later raised the possibility that they had in fact landed on Byan Island. McGee, "To Sink and Swim," 96; Jacobson, *Survivor's Story,* 5, 14.

19. Dean, *Open Water Swimming,* 2, 18, 33, 108, 188–89.

20. Jacobson typescript, 7.

12. Castaways

1. Critchley, *Shipwreck-Survivors,* 71–72.

2. Jacobson typescript, 9.

3. Crowley, Survival Report.

4. Weir and Boyne, *Rising Tide,* 149.

5. McCance, *Hazards to Men in Ships,* 33; Critchely, *Shipwreck-Survivors,* 24–25, 48–49.

6. Gordon L. Rottman, *World War II Pacific Island Guide: A Geo-Military Study* (Westport, Conn.: Greenwood Press, 2002), 307; Robert Ross Smith, *Triumph in the Philippines,* in *United States Army in World War II: The War in the Pacific,* gen. ed. Stetson Conn (Washington, D.C.: Department of the Army, 1963), 583, 589; Walter Karig et al., *Battle Report: Victory in the Pacific* (New York: Rinehart, 1949), 246.

7. King and Whitehall, *Fleet Admiral King,* 97.

8. Dissette and Adamson, *Guerrilla Submarines,* 149–50; Willoughby, *Guerrilla Resistance Movement,* 160.

9. Jacobson, *Survivor's Story,* 17.

10. Walter Karig et al., *Battle Report: The End of an Empire* (New York: Rinehart, 1948), 199. See also McCance, *Hazards to Men in Ships,* 32; Critchley, *Shipwreck-Survivors,* 51–52.

11. Crowley, "Loss of USS *Flier.*" See also *New York Times,* 3 December 1944, 31; USS *Flier* (SS-250), http://ussubvetsofworldwarii.org/ss_submarines/ss250.htm (accessed 19 August 2004).

12. Jacobson typescript, 16.

13. Guerrillas

1. Critchely, *Shipwreck-Survivors,* 62.

2. Crowley, Survival Report; Crowley, "Loss of USS *Flier*"; McGee, "To Sink and Swim," 96–97; Jacobson typescript, 16–18.

3. Vldarico S. Baclagon, *Philippine Campaigns* (Philippine Military Academy, 1952), 262–63; Willoughby, *Guerrilla Resistance Movement*, 46; Dissette and Adamson, *Guerrilla Submarines*, 31; William B. Breuer, *MacArthur's Undercover War: Spies, Saboteurs, Guerrillas, and Secret Missions* (New York: John Wiley and Sons, 1995), 49, 180; Ostlund, *Find 'Em*, 10.

4. Allison Ind, *Allied Intelligence Bureau: Our Secret Weapon in the War against Japan* (New York: David McKay, 1958), 11–12; Allied Intelligence Bureau in Australia during WW2, http://ozatwar.com/sigint/aib .htm (accessed 9 February 2006).

5. Ind, *Allied Intelligence Bureau*, 181–82; Alan Powell, *War by Stealth: Australians and the Allied Intelligence Bureau, 1942–1945* (Melbourne: Melbourne University Press, 1996), 155.

6. Powell, *War by Stealth*, 65, 83.

7. Charles A. Willoughby and John Chamberlain, *MacArthur 1941–1951: Victory in the Pacific* (Melbourne: William Heinemann, 1956), 201–2.

8. Eric Feldt, *The Coast Watchers* (Sydney: Pacific Books, 1946), 16; Dissette and Adamson, *Guerrilla Submarines*, 75–77; Bob Stahl, *No Good to Me Dead: Behind Japanese Lines in the Philippines* (Annapolis, Md.: Naval Institute Press, 1995), 27; Breuer, *MacArthur's Undercover War*, 116; Travis Ingham, *Rendezvous by Submarine: The Story of Charles Parsons and the Guerrilla-Soldiers in the Philippines* (New York: Doubleday, Doran, 1945), 52–53.

9. Gunton, *Dive*, 157; Ingham, *Rendezvous by Submarine*, 181–82; Jones and Nunan, *U.S. Subs Down Under*, 214, 218; Stahl, *No Good to Me Dead*, 191; Allied Warships, *Crevalle* (SS-291), http://uboat.net/ allies/warships/ship/2996.html (accessed 10 November 2005).

10. Layton, *"And I Was There,"* 39, 73; Smith, *Triumph in the Philippines*, 586; Warner, *Secret Forces*, 208–9; Willoughby, *Guerrilla Resistance Movement*, 110, 158–59, 505; Jacobson, *Survivor's Story*, 45, 52.

11. Jacobson typescript, 27. See also Jacobson, *Survivor's Story*, 20.

12. Stahl, *No Good to Me Dead*, 30, 87.

13. Ibid., 79, 141.

14. Willoughby, *Guerrilla Resistance Movement*, 558.

15. Ingham, *Rendezvous by Submarine*, 24–25; Murray, *Reminiscences*, 121; Philippine Scouts, http://www.nationmaster.com/ encyclopedia/Philippine-Scouts (accessed 19 October 2004); USAFFE, http://www.fact-index.com/u/us/usaffe.html (accessed 22 October 2004).

16. Jacobson typescript, 29.

14. Brooke's Point

1. Willoughby, *Guerrilla Resistance Movement,* 508, 572.

2. Jacobson typescript, 28.

3. Hampton Sides, *Ghost Soldiers: The Forgotten Epic Story of World War II's Most Dramatic Mission* (New York: Random House, 2001), 11, 14, 17; Petty, *At War in the Pacific,* 147–48; Morris D. Coppersmith, When Victory Is Ours: Letters Home from the South Pacific 1943–1945, http://www.topshot.com/dh/Victory.html (accessed 13 December 2005); Palawan Massacre, http://www.aiipowmia.com/inter23/in101003palawan.html (accessed 29 September 2004).

4. Rottman, *World War II Pacific Island Guide,* 307; Willoughby, *Guerrilla Resistance Movement,* 64, 505, 508, 558.

5. Jacobson typescript, 29.

6. Stahl, *No Good to Me Dead,* 26; 978th Signal Services Company based at Camp Tabragalba, http://home.st.net.au/~dunn/sigint/978thsig.htm (accessed 9 February 2006); Cacabelos Home Page, http://www.geocities.com/Colosseum/Track/3059/Rufinopart3.html (accessed 9 February 2006).

7. Jacobson, *Survivor's Story,* 53–54.

8. Stahl, *No Good to Me Dead,* 76; Crowley, "Loss of the USS *Flier*"; Carol Stokes, Island-Hopping in the Rainforest: The Signal Corps and the Pacific Front, http://www.gordon.army.mil.ac/WWII/Pacific.htm (accessed 9 February 2006).

9. Quoted in Willoughby, *Guerrilla Resistance Movement,* 159.

10. R. C. Burns, "Palawan Rescue," *U.S. Naval Institute Proceedings,* June 1950, 652–53, *Flier* Scrapbook, SFM.

11. Quoted in Willoughby, *Guerrilla Resistance Movement,* 160.

12. Ibid., 159–60; Earl Baumgart to USS *Bowfin* Submarine Museum, 26 January 1992, *Flier* File, UBSM; *Looking Aft,* vol. 8, no. 1 (March 2001): 3, *Flier* Scrapbook, SFM; History of USS *Redfin* (SS 272), USS *Redfin* Scrapbook, SFM.

13. Baumgart to *Bowfin* Submarine Museum, 26 January 1992.

14. Crowley, Survival Report; Burns, "Palwan Rescue," 652–53; USS *Flier* (SS-250), http://ussubvetsofworldwarii.org/ss_submarines/ss250.htm (accessed 19 August 2004).

15. USS *Redfin*

1. Kaplan, *Run Silent,* 43; Godfrey interview.

2. M. H. Austin File, UBSM; Obituaries—WW2 Veterans, Wild Bill Guarnere Community, http://forums.wildbillguarnere.com/ (accessed 26

April 2006); Naval Submarine League, NSL Update 08–24–2005, http://
www.navalsubleague.com/sub_news/08–24–05.htm (accessed 26 April
2006).

3. Allyn D. Nevitt, IJN Akigumo: Tabular Record of Movement,
http://www.combinedfleet.com/akigum_t.htm (accessed 27 April 2006).

4. Fremantle, 1944–1945, box 82, folder 7, CBC; USS *Redfin* File,
UBSM; Blair, *Silent Victory*, 619.

5. Dissette and Adamson, *Guerrilla Submarines*, 125–26; Blair, *Silent Victory*, 650; William J. Ruhe, *War in the Boats: My World War II Submarine Battles* (Washington, D.C.: Brassey's, 1994), 200; Milton, *Subs against the Rising Sun*, 172.

6. USS *Redfin* Fourth War Patrol Report, 13 August 1944, UBSM;
Lott, *Most Dangerous Sea*, 212.

7. USS *Redfin* Fourth War Patrol Report, 22 August 1944.

8. Holmes, *Undersea Victory*, 381.

9. Jones and Nunan, *U.S. Subs Down Under*, 131–32.

10. G. B. Courtney, *Silent Feet: The History of "Z" Special Operations, 1942–1945* (McCrae, Australia: R. J. and S. P. Austin, 1993), 28.

16. Evacuees

1. Parillo, *Japanese Merchant Marine*, 169, 174, 182.

2. Action Report of the USS *Redfin* Regarding Its Special Mission
23–31 August 1944, Record Group 38, NARA; Crowley, "Loss of USS
Flier"; Peter Amunrud, "Men against the Sea: The Sinking of the USS *Flier* SS-250," *American Submariner* 4 (October–November 1997): 14–15,
23.

3. Jacobson typescript, 31.

4. Ibid., 33; Action Report of the USS *Redfin*.

5. Jacobson typescript, 33–34; Amunrud, "Men against the Sea."

6. Crowley, "Loss of USS *Flier*."

7. Courtney, *Silent Feet*, 4, 139.

8. Ralph Christie to Thomas Kinkaid, 29 August 1944, box 65, folder 6, CBC; A. B. Feuer, *Commando! The M/Z Unit's Secret War against Japan* (Westport, Conn.: Praeger, 1996), 41.

9. Dissette and Adamson, *Guerrilla Submarines*, 148; Courtney, *Silent Feet*, 140.

17. On Board

1. Christley, *U.S. Submarines*, 46–47.

2. Action Report of the USS *Redfin* Regarding Its Special Mission;

USS *Redfin* Fourth War Patrol Report, 31 August 1944; Baumgart to *Bowfin* Submarine Museum, 26 January 1992.

3. Stahl, *No Good to Me Dead,* 29.

4. See, for example, Henry and Keith, *Gallant Lady,* 218; Ruiz, *Luck of the Draw,* 189.

5. Ingham, *Rendezvous by Submarine,* 187–88, 194–95.

6. Critchley, *Shipwreck-Survivors,* 63, 72.

7. Jacobson typescript, 36.

8. Dissette and Adamson, *Guerrilla Submarines,* 236; Ind, *Allied Intelligence Bureau,* 198.

9. Willoughby, *Guerrilla Resistance Movement,* 209–10; Ingham, *Rendezvous by Submarine,* 195.

10. Gleason, "Diary of a War Patrol—USS *Gurnard*"; Bartholomew, Fremantle Submarine Base; Frame, *Pacific Partners,* 74.

11. USS *Redfin* Fourth War Patrol Report, 5–6 September 1944; Division of Naval History, *Redfin* File, UBSM.

12. Feuer, *Commando,* 41.

13. USS *Redfin* Fourth War Patrol Report, Health, Food and Habitability.

14. Milton, *Subs against the Rising Sun,* 172.

15. Jacobson typescript, 36.

16. Jacobson, *Survivor's Story,* 32.

17. Crowley narrative; Schratz, *Submarine Commander,* 180, 182; Paine, *Transpacific Voyage,* 14; Mansfield, *Cruisers for Breakfast,* 62; Jones and Nunan, *U.S. Subs Down Under,* 211.

18. Jacobson typescript, 36.

18. Fallout

1. Ruhe, *War in the Boats,* 266–68; Parillo, *Japanese Merchant Marine,* 131.

2. William R. McCants, *War Patrols of the USS* Flasher (Chapel Hill, N.C.: Professional Press, 1994), 180–81.

3. Fife reminiscences, 4, 15, 46–47, 53, 84, 135, 238–40; Morison, *History of U.S. Naval Operations,* 281.

4. Holmes, *The Last Patrol,* 32, 34, 37; Powell, *War by Stealth,* 65; Fife reminiscences, 332–33; Ostlund, *Find 'Em,* 195; DeRose, *Unrestricted Warfare,* 72.

5. Jones and Nunan, *U.S. Subs Down Under,* 180.

6. Ibid., 109.

7. Fife reminiscences, 334.

8. Christie interview.

9. Blair, *Silent Victory,* 327.

10. Christie interview.

11. Fife reminiscences, 350.

12. Bartholomew, Fremantle Submarine Base.

13. Andrews interview; Nichols interview; Robert Dornin interview, box 97, folder 11, CBC; Frederick Warder interview, box 99, folders 21–22, CBC.

14. Quoted in Blair, *Silent Victory,* 376.

15. Ralph Christie to T. C. Kinkaid, 29 August 1944, box 65, folder 6, CBC.

16. Ralph Christie to Clay Blair, 19 June 1972, box 65, folder 7, CBC.

19. Bend of the Road

1. Biographical Files on Rear Admiral Freeland Allan Daubin, Naval Historical Center, Washington Navy Yard, Washington, D.C.

2. Alden, *Fleet Submarine,* 83, 86; Weir and Boyne, *Rising Tide,* 188.

3. C. A. Lockwood to F. A. Daubin, 8 September 1944, box 57, folder 3, CBC.

4. Peter Marks interview, 7 August 2006 (Perth); T. S. Louch, *The History of the Weld Club (1871–1950)* (Perth: Weld Club, 1980); Paul De Serville, *3 Barrack Street: The Weld Club, 1871–2001* (Wahroonga, Australia: Helicon Press, 2003).

5. Gugliotta, *Pigboat 39,* 178.

6. Louch, *History of the Weld Club,* 150–51.

7. Christie interview.

8. Nichols interview.

9. *West Australian,* 28 June 1943, 2; *Perth Daily News,* 28 June 1943, 4; H. J. Gibney and Ann G. Smith, eds., *A Biographical Register 1788–1939,* vol. 1 (Canberra: Australian Dictionary of Biography, 1987).

10. Christie interview.

11. Dornin interview; Andrews interview; Rear Admiral Ralph Waldo Christie, box 59, folder 8, CBC.

12. Christie interview.

20. Inquiry

1. Nichols interview; Christie interview; Andrews interview.

2. Donald I. Thomas, "Rocks and Shoals," *Shipmate* 54, no. 7 (September 1991); Department of the Navy, *Articles for the Government of*

the United States Navy (Washington, D.C.: U.S. Government Printing Office, 1932), article 57, http://www.history.navy.mil/faqs/faq59-7.htm (accessed 8 December 2005); Buell, *Master of Sea Power*, 346–47.

3. Gleason, "Diary of a War Patrol—USS *Gurnard.*"

4. Andrews interview.

5. Ralph Christie to T. C. Kinkaid, 29 August 1944, box 65, folder 6, CBC.

6. Andrews interview.

7. Ralph Christie to Clay Blair, 19 June 1972, box 65, folder 7, CBC.

8. Blair, *Silent Victory*, 715.

9. Christie to Kinkaid, 29 August 1944.

10. Statement of Rear Admiral R. W. Christie before Rear Admiral F. A. Daubin, Investigating Officer, box 65, folder 6, CBC.

11. Blair, *Silent Victory*, 286, 716.

12. L. E. Denfeld to R. W. Christie, 3 August 1943, box 65, folder 6, CBC; Blair, *Silent Victory*, 341, 368.

13. Lockwood to Christie, 20 August 1943, box 65, folder 6, CBC; interview notes, box 59, folder 8, CBC.

14. Nichols interview.

15. Christie to Kinkaid, 29 August 1944.

16. Crowley, "Loss of the USS *Flier.*"

17. Statement of Christie before Daubin.

18. Christie to Kinkaid, 29 August 1944.

19. Christie to Blair, 19 June 1972.

20. Cutter, *Reminiscences*, 271.

21. C. A. Lockwood to T. C. Kinkaid, 12 September 1944, box 57, folder 3, CBC.

22. Christie to Kinkaid, 29 August 1944.

23. Mansfield, *Cruisers for Breakfast*, 179; Morison, *History of U.S. Naval Operations*, 173.

24. Christie interview.

25. Fife reminiscences, 426–27.

26. Stanton, *In Harm's Way*, 8, 247–48, 253; Buell, *Master of Sea Power*, 348–49.

27. Maas, *Terrible Hours*, 281–83.

28. Van Der Vat, *Stealth at Sea*, 299.

21. Report Incognito

1. Christie interview; Nichols interview.

2. Ralph Christie to Clay Blair, 19 June 1972, box 65, folder 7, CBC.

3. Statement of Christie before Daubin.

4. Andrews interview.

5. Cutter, *Reminiscences,* 514; Ostlund, *Find 'Em,* 18.

6. Robert E. Dornin, *Reminiscences of Captain Robert E. Dornin* (Annapolis, Md.: U.S. Naval Institute, 1987), 1, 3, 15; Dornin interview; Parrish, *The Submarine,* 317; Holmes, *Undersea Victory,* 1–2, 17–18; Van Der Vat, *Stealth at Sea,* 277, 279.

7. C. A. Lockwood to R. W. Christie, 25 July 1944, box 65, folder 6, CBC.

8. Kaplan, *Run Silent,* 80; King and Whitehill, *Fleet Admiral King,* 8, 282, 322, 393–94; Buell, *Master of Sea Power,* xxiii, 62, 64.

9. Buell, *Master of Sea Power,* 89, 452.

10. Dornin interview.

11. Quoted in Van Der Vat, *Stealth at Sea,* 313.

12. Quoted in Perras, *Stepping Stones to Nowhere,* 66.

13. Andrews interview; also quoted in Blair, *Silent Victory,* 716.

14. Buell, *Master of Sea Power,* 347–48, 350; Stanton, *In Harm's Way,* 249; King and Whitehill, *Fleet Admiral King,* 146–47; Layton, *"And I Was There,"* 337–39.

15. L. E. Denfeld to C. A. Lockwood, 15 November 1944, box 57, folder 3, CBC.

16. Biographical files on Rear Admiral Freeland A. Daubin.

17. Christie interview; Clark G. Reynolds, *Famous American Admirals* (New York: Van Nostrand Reinhold, 1978), 69.

18. See Blair, *Silent Victory,* 812–14.

19. Christie to Blair, 20 June 1972.

20. Fife reminiscences, 405–6.

21. McCants, *War Patrols of the USS* Flasher, 180; C. A. Lockwood to T. C. Kinkaid, 12 September 1944, box 57, folder 3, CBC.

22. Back in the USA

1. R. C. Burns, "Palawan Rescue," *U.S. Naval Institute Proceedings,* June 1950, 652–53.

2. Cutter, *Reminiscences,* 141–42, 283, 286.

3. Perras, *Stepping Stones to Nowhere,* 159.

4. See, for example, Ruiz, *Luck of the Draw,* 264–65.

5. Eli Ginzberg et al., *The Lost Divisions* (New York: Columbia University Press, 1959), 128; Jenny Edkins, *Trauma and the Politics of Memory* (Cambridge: Cambridge University Press, 2003), 2–3, 46.

6. See Edgar Jones and Simon Wessely, *Shell Shock to PTSD: Military Psychiatry from 1900 to the Gulf War* (New York: Psychology Press, 2005), 87, 98–99, 173–74, 212.

7. See P. Post et al., *Disaster Ritual: Explorations of an Emerging Ritual Repertoire* (Leuven, Belgium: Peeters, 2003), 227, 264, 269; Eli Ginzberg, John L. Herma, and Sol W. Ginzberg, *Psychiatry and Military Manpower Policy: A Reappraisal of the Experience in World War II* (New York: King's Crown Press and Columbia University, 1953), 30; Ginzberg et al., *Lost Divisions*, 62.

8. Jacobson to author, 12 May 2006; Jacobson interview, 19 May 2006.

9. C. A. Lockwood to T. C. Kinkaid, 12 September 1944, box 57, folder 3, CBC.

10. Quoted in Maas, *Terrible Hours*, 307. See also Damousi, *The Labour of Loss*, 9.

11. L. E. Denfeld to Mr. and Mrs. A. E. Jacobson Sr., 14 September 1944, in Jacobson, *Survivor's Story*, 58.

12. Jacobson, *Survivor's Story*, 32.

13. Biographical files on Captain John D. Crowley, Naval Historical Center, Washington Navy Yard, Washington, D.C.

23. Next of Kin

1. A. C. Jacobs to Lt. Gordon, 13 September 1944, Casualty Reports of USS *Flier* from the Casualty Assistance Branch, Bureau of Naval Personnel, Record Group 38, NARA.

2. C. C. Burlingame to Chief of Naval Personnel (Casualty and Allotment Section), 10 October 1944, NARA.

3. Cutter, *Reminiscences*, 126.

4. Mansfield, *Cruisers for Breakfast*, 205, 207–8, 226–27.

5. Schratz, *Submarine Commander*, 65–66.

6. See Paul Fussell, *Wartime: Understanding and Behavior in the Second World War* (New York: Oxford University Press, 1989), 145.

7. See Kaplan, *Run Silent*, 87–88; Spector, *At War at Sea*, 341.

8. Godfrey interview.

9. Thomson interview.

10. Mansfield, *Cruisers for Breakfast*, 207–9.

11. Royle interview.

12. Cutter, *Reminiscences*, 98–99.

13. C. A. Lockwood to Virgie Dealey, 17 October 1944, box 57, folder 3, CBC.

14. C. W. Nimitz to G. B. Dealey, undated, ibid.

15. Nichols interview; Buell, *Master of Sea Power*, 414; Ralph Christie to Clay Blair, 20 June 1972, box 65, folder 7, CBC.

16. John D. Crowley to Albert C. Jacobs, 14 December 1944, NARA.

17. Superseding Statement Concerning Finding of Death, Walter W. Finke to Chief of Naval Personnel, 11 January 1946, NARA. See also Fife reminiscences, 438.

18. Edkins, *Trauma and the Politics of Memory,* 98; Neil Hanson, *The Unknown Soldier: The Story of the Missing of the Great War* (London: Doubleday, 2005), 398, 417.

19. See Joy Damousi, *Living with the Aftermath: Trauma, Nostalgia and Grief in Post-war Australia* (Melbourne: Cambridge University Press, 2001), 67.

20. Schratz, *Submarine Commander,* 156.

21. Adams, "USS Tang Survivors."

22. J. D. Crowley to Chief of Naval Personnel, 5 November 1947; J. R. Carnes to Mrs. Paul Knapp, 19 November 1947, NARA.

23. *New London Day,* 16 April 1946, *Flier* Scrapbook, SFM.

Epilogue

1. History of the U.S.S. *Irex* SS-482 (1945–1946), http://www .hartford-hwp.com/Irex/docs/history (accessed 19 August 2004); Tench Class Submarines, http://www.usstorsk.org/tench/423class.htm (accessed 13 April 2006).

2. *New London Day,* 4 January 1946, *Flier* Scrapbook, SFM.

3. Biographical files on Captain John D. Crowley; John D. Crowley Military Personnel Records.

4. See Jones and Wessely, *Shell Shock,* 210.

5. Jacobson, *Survivor's Story,* 56; *Looking Aft,* vol. 8, no. 1 (March 2001), *Redfin* Scrapbook, SFM.

6. Naval Submarine League, http://www.navalsubleague.com/sub_news/08-24-05.htm (accessed 26 April 2006); Obituaries—WW2 Veterans, http://forums.wildbillguarnere.com/ (accessed 26 April 2006).

7. Jacobson interview, 19 May 2006; Jacobson to author, 12 May 2006.

8. Earl Baumgart to I. J. Galantin, 10 November 1992, *Flier* File, UBSM; Aldona Sendzikas to John D. Crowley, 17 January 1992, ibid.

9. Jacobson, *Survivor's Story,* 5, 32, 41, 71–72; Jacobson to author, 22 February, 12 May 2006; Jacobson interview.

Bibliography

Archives

Clay Blair Collection, American Heritage Center, University of Wyoming, Laramie

Charles Andrews, taped interview, box 96, folders 15–17
Ralph Waldo Christie, taped interview, box 97, folders 2–5
Rear Admiral Ralph Waldo Christie, box 59, folder 8; box 65, folder 6
Robert Dornin, taped interview, box 97, folder 11
Fremantle, 1944–1945, box 82, folder 7
Frank Lynch, taped interview, box 98, folder 9
Philip Nichols, taped interview, box 99, folder 13
Skippers of U.S. World War II Pacific Ocean Submarine Patrols—John Daniel Crowley and James Liddell, box 67, folder 2
Frederick Warder, taped interview, box 99, folders 21–22

Columbia University, Oral History Research Office, New York

Reminiscences of Admiral James Fife, Oral History Memoir transcript, 1962

National Archives and Records Administration, College Park, Maryland

Action Report of the USS *Redfin* Regarding Its Special Mission 23–31 August 1944; Records of the Office of the Chief of Naval Operations, Record Group 38
Casualty reports of USS *Flier* from the Casualty Assistance Branch, Bureau of Naval Personnel; Records of the Office of the Chief of Naval Operations, Record Group 38
Chronological Narrative of Second War Patrol of USS *Flier* in Philippines Area [submarine proceeding on surface off Comiran Island when it exploded probably as a result of striking a mine, on 13 August 1944], Survival Report; Records of the Office of the Chief of Naval Operations, Record Group 38

191

National Personnel Records Center, St. Louis, Missouri
John D. Crowley Military Personnel Records

Naval Historical Center, Washington Navy Yard, Washington, D.C.
Biographical files on Captain John D. Crowley
Biographical files on Rear Admiral Freeland Allan Daubin

Office of the Judge Advocate General, Department of the Navy, Washington, D.C.
Final Investigative Report into the Grounding of the USS *Flier* (SS-250) on January 16, 1944

Submarine Force Museum, Groton, Connecticut
USS *Flier* Scrapbook
USS *Redfin* Scrapbook

USS *Bowfin* Submarine Museum, Pearl Harbor, Hawaii
Benjamin E. Adams Jr. File
Marshall H. Austin File
John D. Crowley File
Manning M. Kimmel File
USS *Flier* File
USS *Flier* First War Patrol Report
USS *Rasher* File
USS *Redfin* File
USS *Redfin* Fourth War Patrol Report
USS *Robalo* File
USS *S-28* First to Fifth War Patrol Reports

Personal Interviews

Alvin E. Jacobson, interview with author, 19 May 2006 (and additional correspondence with author)
Peter Marks, interview with author, 7 August 2006, Perth
Norma Black Royle, interview with Alan Royle, 29 November 2005
Elizabeth Thomson, interview with author, 30 September 2006, Perth

Books and Articles

Adams, Cindy. "USS Tang Survivors." *Polaris,* February 1981. http://www.subvetpaul.com/SAGA_2_81.htm (accessed 1 July 2005).

Alden, John D. *The Fleet Submarine in the U.S. Navy: A Design and Construction History.* London: Arms and Armour Press, 1979.
———. *U.S. Submarine Attacks during World War II.* Annapolis, Md.: Naval Institute Press, 1989.
Amunrud, Peter. "Men against the Sea: The Sinking of the USS *Flier* SS-250." *American Submariner* 4 (October–November 1997): 14–15, 23.
Baclagon, Vldarico S. *Philippine Campaigns.* Philippine Military Academy, 1952.
Bartholomew, Bart. "Submarine School." *Polaris,* April 1994. http://www.subvetpaul.com/SAGA_4_94.htm (accessed 1 July 2005).
Beaumont, Joan, ed. *Australia's War: 1939–45.* Sydney: Allen and Unwin, 1996.
Bernstein, Jeremy. "The Secrets of the Bomb." *New York Review of Books,* 25 May 2006, 41–44.
Bicheno, Hugh. *Midway.* London: Cassell, 2001.
Blair, Clay Jr. *Silent Victory: The U.S. Submarine War against Japan.* 1975. Reprint, Annapolis, Md.: Naval Institute Press, 2001.
Boyd, Carl, and Akihiko Yoshida. *The Japanese Submarine Force and World War II.* Shrewsbury, U.K.: Airlife, 1995.
Breuer, William B. *MacArthur's Undercover War: Spies, Saboteurs, Guerrillas, and Secret Missions.* New York: John Wiley and Sons, 1995.
Budiansky, Stephen. *Battle of Wits: The Complete Story of Codebreaking in World War II.* London: Viking, 2000.
Buell, Thomas B. *Master of Sea Power: A Biography of Fleet Admiral Ernest J. King.* Boston: Little, Brown, 1980.
Burns, R. C. "Palwan Rescue." *U.S. Naval Institute Proceedings,* June 1950.
Christley, Jim. *U.S. Submarines 1941–1945.* New York: Osprey, 2006.
Clary, Jack. "Ballfield to Battlefield." *Navy History,* October 2004.
Courtney, G. B. *Silent Feet: The History of "Z" Special Operations, 1942–1945.* McCrae, Australia: R. J. and S. P. Austin, 1993.
Cressman, Robert J., et al. *"A Glorious Page in Our History": The Battle of Midway, 4–6 June 1942.* Missoula, Mont.: Pictorial Histories, 1990.
Critchley, Macdonald. *Shipwreck-Survivors: A Medical Study.* London: J. and A. Churchill, 1943.
Crowley, John D. (as reported to Bill Wolfe). "Loss of USS *Flier.*" *Polaris,* June 1981. http://www.subvetpaul.com/SAGA_6_81.htm (accessed 1 July 2005).
Cutter, Slade D. *The Reminiscences of Captain Slade D. Cutter.* Interviewed by Paul Stillwell. Annapolis, Md.: U.S. Naval Institute, 1985.

Damousi, Joy. *The Labour of Loss: Mourning, Memory and Wartime Bereavement in Australia*. Cambridge: Cambridge University Press, 1999.
———. *Living with the Aftermath: Trauma, Nostalgia and Grief in Postwar Australia*. Melbourne: Cambridge University Press, 2001.
Dean, Penny Lee. *Open Water Swimming*. Champaign, Ill.: Human Kinetics, 1998.
DeRose, James F. *Unrestricted Warfare: How a New Breed of Officers Led the Submarine Force to Victory in World War II*. New York: John Wiley and Sons, 2000.
De Serville, Paul. *3 Barrack Street: The Weld Club 1871–2001*. Wahroonga, Australia: Helicon Press, 2003.
Dissette, Edward, and H. C. Adamson. *Guerrilla Submarines*. New York: Ballantine Books, 1972.
Dornin, Robert E. *Reminiscences of Captain Robert E. Dornin*. Annapolis, Md.: U.S. Naval Institute, 1987.
Dower, John W. *War without Mercy: Race and Power in the Pacific War*. New York: Pantheon Books, 1986.
Dowson, John. *Old Fremantle: Photographs 1850–1950*. Perth: University of Western Australia Press, 2003.
Edkins, Jenny. *Trauma and the Politics of Memory*. Cambridge: Cambridge University Press, 2003.
Edwards, John. *Curtin's Gift: Reinterpreting Australia's Greatest Prime Minister*. Sydney: Allen and Unwin, 2005.
Enright, Joseph F., with James W. Ryan. *Shinano! The Sinking of Japan's Secret Supership*. London: Bodley Head, 1987.
Feldt, Eric. *The Coast Watchers*. Sydney: Pacific Books, 1946.
Feuer, A. B. *Commando! The M/Z Unit's Secret War against Japan*. Westport, Conn.: Praeger, 1996.
Frame, Tom. *Pacific Partners: A History of Australian-American Naval Relations*. Sydney: Hodder and Stroughton, 1992.
Friedman, Norman. *Submarine Design and Development*. London: Conway Maritime, 1984.
Fussell, Paul. *Wartime: Understanding and Behavior in the Second World War*. New York: Oxford University Press, 1989.
Galantin, I. J. *Take Her Deep! A Submarine against Japan in World War II*. Chapel Hill, N.C.: Algonquin Books, 1987.
Gibney, Frank, ed. *Senso: The Japanese Remember the Pacific War*. Translated by Beth Cary. London: M. E. Sharpe, 1995.
Gibney, H. J., and Ann G. Smith, eds. *A Biographical Register 1788–1939*. Canberra: Australian Dictionary of Biography, 1987.
Ginzberg, Eli, John L. Herma, and Sol W. Ginzberg. *Psychiatry and Military Manpower Policy: A Reappraisal of the Experience in*

World War II. New York: King's Crown Press and Columbia University, 1953.

Ginzberg, Eli, et al. *The Lost Divisions.* New York: Columbia University Press, 1959.

Gleason, Bill. "Diary of a War Patrol—USS *Gurnard* (SS-254)." *Polaris,* June 1985. http://www.subvetpaul.com/SAGA_6_85.htm (accessed 1 July 2005).

Gray, Edwin. *Few Survived: A Comprehensive Survey of Submarine Accidents and Disasters.* London: Leo Cooper, 1986.

Gugliotta, Bobette. *Pigboat 39: An American Sub Goes to War.* Lexington: University Press of Kentucky, 1984.

Gunton, Michael. *Dive! Dive! Dive! Submarines at War.* London: Constable, 2003.

Hailey, Foster. *Pacific Battle Line.* New York: Macmillan, 1944.

Hamilton, James W., and William J. Bolce Jr. *Gateway to Victory: The Wartime Story of the San Francisco Army Port of Embarkation.* Stanford, Calif.: Stanford University Press, 1946.

Hanson, Neil. *The Unknown Solider: The Story of the Missing of the Great War.* London: Doubleday, 2005.

Healey, Mark. *Midway 1942: Turning Point in the Pacific.* 1993. Reprint, Oxford: Osprey, 2004.

Henry, Ken, and Don Keith. *Gallant Lady: A Biography of the USS* Archerfish. New York: Tom Doherty Associates, 2004.

Hill, A. J. *Under Pressure: The Final Voyage of Submarine S-Five.* New York: New American Library, 2002.

Hodghin, Katherine, and Susannah Radstone, eds. *Contested Pasts: The Politics of Memory.* London: Routledge, 2003.

Holmes, Harry. *The Last Patrol.* Annapolis, Md.: Naval Institute Press, 1994.

Holmes, W. J. *Undersea Victory: The Influence of Submarine Operations on the War in the Pacific.* New York: Doubleday, 1966.

Howarth, Stephen. *To Shining Sea: A History of the United States Navy, 1774–1991.* New York: Random House, 1991.

Hoyt, Edwin. *Bowfin: The Story of One of America's Fabled Fleet Submarines in World War II.* New York: Van Nostrand Reinhold, 1983.

Ind, Allison. *Allied Intelligence Bureau: Our Secret Weapon in the War against Japan.* New York: David McKay, 1958.

Ingham, Travis. *Rendezvous by Submarine: The Story of Charles Parsons and the Guerrilla-Soldiers in the Philippines.* New York: Doubleday, Doran, 1945.

Jacobson, Alvin. *Survivor's Story: Submarine USS* Flier. 1997. Revised 2002. Self-published.

Jones, David, and Peter Nunan. *U.S. Subs Down Under: Brisbane, 1942–1945*. Annapolis, Md.: Naval Institute Press, 2005.

Jones, Edgar, and Simon Wessely. *Shell Shock to PTSD: Military Psychiatry from 1900 to the Gulf War*. New York: Psychology Press, 2005.

Kaplan, Philip. *Run Silent*. Annapolis, Md.: Naval Institute Press, 2002.

Karig, Walter, and Eric Purdon. *Battle Report: Pacific War, Middle Phase*. New York: Rinehart, 1947.

Karig, Walter, et al. *Battle Report: The End of an Empire*. New York: Rinehart, 1948.

———. *Battle Report: Victory in the Pacific*. New York: Rinehart, 1949.

Keith, Don. *In the Course of Duty: The Heroic Mission of the USS Batfish*. New York: NAL Caliber, 2005.

Kimmett, Larry, and Margaret Regis. *U.S. Submarines in World War II: An Illustrated History*. Seattle: Navigator Publishing, 1996.

King, Ernest J., and Walter Muir Whitehill. *Fleet Admiral King: A Naval Record*. London: Eyre and Spottiswoode, 1953.

Layton, Edwin T. *"And I Was There": Pearl Harbor and Midway—Breaking the Secrets*. 1985. Reprint, Annapolis, Md.: Naval Institute Press, 2006.

Lotchin, Roger. "Historians and the Embattled Greatest Generation: Turning the Good War Bad?" Unpublished address, 2005.

Lott, Arnold S. *Most Dangerous Sea: A History of Mine Warfare, and an Account of U.S. Navy Mine Warfare Operations in World War II and Korea*. Annapolis, Md.: U.S. Naval Institute Press, 1959.

Louch, T. S. *The History of the Weld Club (1871–1950)*. Perth: Weld Club, 1980.

Maas, Peter. *The Terrible Hours: The Man behind the Greatest Submarine Rescue in History*. New York: Harper Torch, 1999.

Mack, William P., and Royal W. Connell. *Naval Ceremonies, Customs and Traditions*. Annapolis, Md.: Naval Institute Press, 1980.

Mansfield, John G., Jr. *Cruisers for Breakfast: War Patrols of the U.S.S. Darter and U.S.S. Dace*. Tacoma, Wash.: Media Center Publishing, 1997.

McCance, R. A., et al. *The Hazards to Men in Ships Lost at Sea, 1940–1944*. London: His Majesty's Stationery Office, 1956.

McCants, William R. *War Patrols of the USS Flasher*. Chapel Hill, N.C.: Professional Press, 1994.

McDaniel, J. T., ed. *U.S.S. Wahoo (SS-238) American Submarine Patrol Reports*. Riverdale, Ga.: Riverdale Books, 2003.

McGee, Eugene D. "To Sink and Swim: The USS *Flier*." *Submarine Review*, October 1996, 94–98.

McKee, Christopher. *Sober Men and True: Sailor Lives in the Royal Navy, 1900–1945*. Cambridge, Mass.: Harvard University Press, 2002.

Michno, Gregory F. *USS* Pampanito: *Killer-Angel.* Norman: University of Oklahoma Press, 2000.

Milton, Keith M. *Subs against the Rising Sun.* Las Cruces, N.M.: Yucca Tree Press, 2000.

Ministry of Defence (Navy). *War with Japan.* Vol. 6, *The Advance to Japan.* London: Her Majesty's Stationery Office, 1995.

Moore, Jeffrey M. *Spies for Nimitz: Joint Military Intelligence in the Pacific War.* Annapolis, Md.: Naval Institute Press, 2004.

Morison, Samuel Eliot. *History of the United States Naval Operations in World War II.* Vol. 12, *Leyte June 1944–January 1945.* London: Oxford University Press, 1958.

Murray, Stuart S. *The Reminiscences of Admiral Stuart S. Murray.* Interviewed by Etta-Belle Kitchen. 1974. Reprint, Annapolis, Md.: U.S. Naval Institute, 2001.

Ostlund, Mike. *Find 'Em, Chase 'Em, Sink 'Em: The Mysterious Loss of the WWII Submarine USS* Gudgeon. Guilford, Ccnn.: Lyons Press, 2006.

Paine, T. O. *The Transpacific Voyage of His Imperial Japanese Majesty's Submarine I-400 (Tom Paine's Journal, July–Dec. 1945).* Self-published, 1984.

Parillo, Mark P. *The Japanese Merchant Marine in World War II.* Annapolis, Md.: Naval Institute Press, 1993.

Parrish, Thomas. *The Submarine: A History.* London: Viking Penguin, 2004.

Patric, James H. *To War in a Tin Can: A Memoir of World War II aboard a Destroyer.* Jefferson, N.C.: McFarland, 2004.

Perras, Galen Roger. *Stepping Stones to Nowhere: The Aleutian Islands, Alaska, and American Military Strategy, 1867–1945.* Vancouver, B.C.: UBC Press, 2003.

Petty, Bruce M. *At War in the Pacific: Personal Accounts of World War II Navy and Marine Corps Officers.* Jefferson, N.C.: McFarland, 2006.

Polmar, Norman, and Dorr B. Carpenter. *Submarines of the Imperial Japanese Navy, 1904–1945.* London: Conway Maritime Press, 1986.

Post, P., et al. *Disaster Ritual: Explorations of an Emerging Ritual Repertoire.* Leuven, Belgium: Peeters, 2003.

Potter, E. B., and Chester W. Nimitz, eds. *The Great Sea War: The Story of Naval Action in World War II.* Englewood Cliffs, N.J.: Prentice-Hall, 1960.

Powell, Alan. *War by Stealth: Australians and the Allied Intelligence Bureau, 1942–1945.* Melbourne: Melbourne University Press, 1996.

Reynolds, Clark G. *Famous American Admirals.* New York: Van Nostrand Reinhold, 1978.

Rottman, Gordon L. *World War II Pacific Island Guide: A Geo-Military Study.* Westport, Conn.: Greenwood Press, 2002.

Ruhe, William J. *War in the Boats: My World War II Submarine Battles.* Washington, D.C.: Brassey's, 1994.

Ruiz, C. Kenneth, with John Bruning. *The Luck of the Draw: The Memoir of a World War II Submariner.* St. Paul, Minn.: Zenith Press, 2005.

Schratz, Paul R. *Submarine Commander: A Story of World War II and Korea.* Lexington: University Press of Kentucky, 1988.

Sherriff, Jacqui. "Fremantle South Slipway: A Vital World War II Defence Facility." *Fremantle Studies* 2, no. 2 (2002): 106–19.

Sides, Hampton. *Ghost Soldiers: The Forgotten Epic Story of World War II's Most Dramatic Mission.* New York: Random House, 2001.

A Small War: Corvettes—The 39 through Fremantle. Perth: West Australian Newspapers, 1991.

Smith, J. Douglas, and Richard Jensen. *World War II on the Web: A Guide to the Very Best Sites.* Wilmington, Del.: SR Books, 2003.

Smith, Robert Ross. *Triumph in the Philippines.* In *United States Army in World War II: The War in the Pacific.* General editor Stetson Conn. Washington, D.C.: Department of the Army, 1963.

Smith, Steven Trent. *The Rescue: A True Story of Courage and Survival in World War II.* New York: John Wiley and Sons, 2001.

Sontag, Sherry, and Christopher Drew. *Blind Man's Bluff: The Untold Story of American Submarine Espionage.* New York: Public Affairs, 1998.

Spector, Ronald H. *At War at Sea: Sailors and Naval Combat in the Twentieth Century.* New York: Viking, 2001.

Stahl, Bob. *You're No Good to Me Dead: Behind Japanese Lines in the Philippines.* Annapolis, Md.: Naval Institute Press, 1995.

Stannard, David E. *Honor Killing: How the Infamous "Massie Affair" Transformed Hawai'i.* New York: Viking, 2005.

Stanton, Doug. *In Harm's Way.* New York: St. Martin's Paperbacks, 2002.

Sterling, Forest J. *Wake of the Wahoo.* Philadelphia: Chilton, 1960.

Sturma, Michael. *Death at a Distance: The Loss of the Legendary USS Harder.* Annapolis, Md.: Naval Institute Press, 2006.

Thomas, Donald I. "Rocks and Shoals." *Shipmate* 54, no. 7 (September 1991). http://www.history.navy.mil/faqs/faq59–6.htm (accessed 8 December 2005).

Tohmatsu, Harso, and H. P. Willmott. *A Gathering Darkness: The Coming of War to the Far East and the Pacific, 1921–1942.* New York: SR Books, 2004.

Tuohy, William. *The Bravest Man: The Story of Richard O'Kane and U.S. Submariners in the Pacific War.* Thrupp Stroud, U.K.: Sutton, 2002.

U.S. Navy Bureau of Ships. *Submarine Material Guide.* Washington, D.C.: U.S. Navy, 1944.

Van Der Vat, Dan. *Stealth at Sea: The History of the Submarine.* London: Orion, 1995.

Walker, David. "Shooting Mabel: Warrior Masculinity and the Asian Invasion." *History Australia* 2, no. 3 (December 2005).

Warner, Philip. *Secret Forces of World War II.* 1985. Reprint, Barnsley, U.K.: Pen and Sword, 2004.

Weir, Gary E., and Walter J. Boyne. *Rising Tide: The Untold Story of the Russian Submarines that Fought the Cold War.* New York: Basic Books, 2003.

Willoughby, Charles A. *The Guerrilla Resistance Movement in the Philippines: 1941–1945.* New York: Vantage Press, 1972.

Willoughby, Charles A., and John Chamberlain. *MacArthur 1941–1951: Victory in the Pacific.* Melbourne: William Heinemann, 1956.

Wood, Adrian, ed. *If This Should Be Farewell: A Family Separated by War.* Fremantle, Australia: Fremantle Arts Centre Press, 2003.

Index

201